基本中国拳法

自卫的哲学艺术

李小龙 著
黄筠 译

北京联合出版公司
Beijing United Publishing Co.,Ltd.

出版前言

李小龙通晓各派武术，深谙东方哲学，是"战无不胜"的功夫之王、万人敬仰的武学宗师，他在武术上的成就震古烁今，堪为后世习武者之楷模。

本书是李小龙生前出版的第一本，也是唯一一本中国武术专著，内容包括李小龙对中国拳法基本姿势、训练方法的精到介绍和中国拳法格斗技巧的模拟展示。作为一个武术天才，李小龙对中国功夫的精髓有着深刻独到的理解，而在这些简洁、清晰的指导背后，凝聚着他最珍贵的习武经验。在李小龙看来，中国功夫最讲究阴阳调和，顺其自然；习练中国拳法的宗旨是强身健体，磨练心智；中国武术的技巧不是以力抵力，而是以退为进，顺势而为，如果企图单纯从力量上对抗或压制对手，不仅收效甚微，还可能伤及自身。这本书完美地展现了李小龙的武术基础，也很好地预示了他之后所独创的的武术道路。毫无疑问，这本书不仅是最权威的中国拳法指导，也是李小龙传奇人生中的一份真实见证。

　　本版完整编排了李小龙亲笔手绘的训练步骤图和独特的手写字体，并将李小龙与众多武术专家的多场景实战模拟照片进行了高清还原，同时收录了李小龙遗孀琳达·李·卡德威尔、爱女李香凝等人的深情回忆文章，力求将一代宗师最纯粹的的功夫世界完美再现于读者面前。在此，出版方要特别向译者黄筠女士和为本书提供了专业建议的史旭光先生表示感谢。

　　除已出版的《李小龙技击法》《生活的艺术家》《截拳道之道》《李小龙基本中国拳法》之外，我们还将引进出版李小龙其他经典原著，敬请期待。

服务热线：133-6631-2326　188-1142-1266

服务信箱：reader@hinabook.com

后浪出版公司

2015年10月

推荐序

《李小龙基本中国拳法》是李小龙生前出版的第一本,也是唯一一本关于中国功夫的专著。小龙自幼在香港习武,此书展现的是他从幼时起到赴美后前五年里所学习到的武术知识。在叶问大师门下,小龙学习了中国传统武术咏春拳,并通过他的自学及与其他武术高手的接触交流,大量学习了其他不同风格的功夫。他做了大量的笔记、剪报和手绘图研究古今不同的功夫流派和兵器,其中一部分内容在这本小册子中也有呈现。

在《李小龙基本中国拳法》出版后的几年里,小龙在武术上的发展方向从传统武术转向专研他自己的拳路,他将其称为"截拳道"或者说"截击来拳之道"。实际上,在之后几年,小龙强烈希望从传统武术中解放自己,为此他要求出版商停止出版此书。

《李小龙基本中国拳法》在小龙去世后重新出版,并一直再版至今日,这是因为人们开始将它奉为经典,并把它视作展现中国功夫与技法的代表之作。这本书向读者展示了李小龙的武术基础,它也是李小龙传奇人生中的一个历史见证。

琳达·李·卡德威尔
2008年

目 录

出版前言 …………………………………………… 1

推荐序 ……………………………………………… 3

导　言 ……………………………………………… 7

第一部分　中国武术的基础 …………………… 1

　　第一章　关于中国功夫　2

　　第二章　几点重要提示　5

　　第三章　基本功夫姿势　7

　　第四章　腰部训练　20

　　第五章　腿部训练　24

　　第六章　功夫中的阴阳哲理　31

第二部分　中国功夫的技术 …………………… 37

　　第七章　中国拳法的实例　38

第八章　不同的功夫风格　82

第九章　还原与见证：李小龙武术习练及照片　92

附　录　回忆李小龙 ……………………………… 119

希望与荣耀：李小龙的自卫术　120

功夫天才李小龙　123

别开生面的中国搏击术　125

李小龙基本中国拳法（英文版）…………………… 127

导　言

中国功夫素为远东武术的核心，它的原理和技巧渗透并影响了其他的东方自卫术。一直以来，由于中国功夫被蒙上了一层极为神秘的面纱，因此它较少为西方世界以及其他东方国家所知。

事实上，中国功夫已有四千年的历史。在古时，功夫是无限制的打斗；但随着时间的推移，历代武术前辈将它逐渐完善，去芜存菁，使其日臻精进。再后来，功夫又融入了解剖学、宗教、心理学，逐渐上升到更高的层面，成为兼具高度科学性和哲学色彩的自卫术，那已是距今两三千年的事了！功夫的宗旨是为了强身健体，磨炼心智和保护自我。它的哲学理念融道学、禅学、易经为一体，包括顺势而为，以退为进，不与对手以力抵力，而是顺应其力等理念。功夫的技巧并非着重于力，而是强调阴阳，即能量守恒和不走极端的中庸之道。这就是为何一个真正的武者既不以力抵力（那样会产生反作用力），也不彻底避让，而是如弹簧般柔韧善变。他寻求顺应对手的攻击——顺其劲力，而非与之相抗。

我曾研习咏春多年，那是朴实无华的武艺。我不再为对手、"自我"或者形式上的技巧等分心。我将对手的技巧化为己物，我的任务仅仅是完善另一半以达到自我合一，我的行动是为了达到无为，即自然地顺应形势，随机应变。以心调意、以意领气、以气催力等训练化无为有，一切顺应自然。

如今，我的一位好友邀请我撰写一本被我长期抛在脑后的功夫书籍。为回应他的期望，我在此书中还挑选了一些我学咏春拳之前所学的其他武术门派的基本技术。尽管功夫的终极追求确实是在精神层面，但磨练技巧是达到这一最终境界的敲门砖。

我要在此强调的是，此书并非是有关正规武术技术的教材，它仅仅囊括了一些基本防守和攻击动作。在不久的将来我从亚洲回来的时候，另一本更为深入的书籍《功夫之道》将出版。

在美国的三年，我见过一些不诚实的"生意人"，其中有美国人也有中国人，他们自诩是功夫领域的专家或高手，但其动作却不与任何门派"雷同"。我希望那些正准备加入这些"门派"的人们睁大眼睛看仔细。此外，还需要补充的一点是，不管是谁读了这本书，他都不会成为一个"危险分子"，也不会在学了三门简易课程后就成为"功夫高手"。

李小龙

第一部分
中国武术的基础

第一章　关于中国功夫

中国功夫基本由以下五个部分组成：

1. 打法（打法）

包括运用掌、拳、膝、肘、肩、臂、头、腿的所有技巧，但是不包括其他流派中特有的技术，比如鹰爪、鹤形拳、螳螂拳等。

2. 踢法（踢法）

包括南北流派踢法中的所有踢击技术。

3. 擒拿（擒拿）

包括七十二种不同的分筋错骨的擒锁技术。

4. 摔法（摔法）

包括三十六种摔法。

5. 武器（武器）

包括十八般兵器。

中国武术南北流派中有众多派别，其中知名的有：

北派：

咏春派八卦（咏春派八卦）

形意（形意）

螳螂（螳螂）

鹰爪派（鹰爪派）

谭腿门（谭腿门）

弹腿门（弹腿门）

北少林（北少林）

罗汉拳（罗汉拳）

迷踪艺（迷踪艺）

西岳华拳（西岳华拳）

查拳（查拳）

猴拳大圣门（猴拳大圣门）

长江派（长江派）

……

南派：

咏春派（咏春派）

南派螳螂（南派螳螂）

白眉派（白眉派）

白鹤派（白鹤派）

南派少林（南派少林）

蔡李佛（蔡李佛）

洪家（洪家）

蔡家（蔡家）

佛家（佛家）

莫家（莫家）

柔功门（柔功门）

李家（李家）

刘家（刘家）

……

这些派别又可分为内家与外家（内家与外家），这里我们不作讨论。

第二章　几点重要提示

1.功夫如行云流水，动作连绵不断。每个动作将止之际，下一手就已跟进。正因如此，读者将会发现中国功夫中的技术会比普通的格斗技术更快。

2.功夫是对意念的训练。在功夫的更高层阶段，达到身心一体尤为重要。对读者而言，需尝试用意念去引导身体的活动。比如，坚信每个技术都将取得令人满意的效果将有助于练习。

3.顺势而为。不要抵抗或强硬地截断对手的拳路。你无需阻断他的力量，而应顺其劲力。换句话说，你应借力打力，把对方的力量反作用于其自身。记住你应根据对手的反应而做出反应，这就是我们为何说"不应以力抵力，而应因势利导"。

4.腰部在功夫技法中极为重要，它在进攻和化解对手攻击上发挥着主要作用。在练习中，练习者需在侧闪之前,先用转腰化解对方的劲力。

5.请记住,学会忍耐比学会进攻更有用。但无论如何,如果你被迫使用武力,那就好好利用它。

第三章　基本功夫姿势

　　功夫中有许多适用于不同情况的基本姿势，其他一些武术流派也有独特的姿势。以下是适用于初学者的十种常见功夫姿势。（注：图中数字为重心在两腿分配的比例。）

图 3-1

1. 马步（马步）

大腿平行于地面，脚尖和膝盖朝前。两脚间距越窄越好。

注意：避免膝盖外张以及身体前倾或后仰。

第一部分　中国武术的基础　　9

图 3-2

2. 弓步（弓步）

重心放在前腿，脚尖稍向内扣，防止被踩，后腿绷直。如图所示，这就是为何这一姿势被称为"弓箭步"。此姿势和马步一样刚劲有力，稳如泰山。

注意：避免后脚跟离地以及前脚掌朝前。

图 3-3

3. 丁 步（丁步）

重心多集中在后腿，前脚点地，随时准备踢击。前膝高于后膝，以护裆部。

注意：避免重心在前腿以及前脚背没有绷直。

第一部分　中国武术的基础　11

图 3-4

4. 虚步（虚步）

丁步的变式，不同之处在于前脚掌略微内扣。

注意：避免重心在前腿。

图3-5

5. 中式（中式）

此势介于马步与虚步之间，较为灵活，多用于自由搏击。前膝略高于后膝。

第一部分　中国武术的基础　13

图3-6

6. 七星（七星）

重心在后脚，前脚脚跟轻点地，脚尖朝上。此姿势多与弓步并用以化解压力。在此姿势中，转腰十分重要。两膝尽量保持在同一水平线上。

图 3-7

7. 拗马（扭马）

两脚交叉。前脚踩实，后脚跟离地。此姿势多用于近距离快速移动。

第一部分　中国武术的基础　15

图 3-8

8. 跪马（跪马）

重心在前支撑腿。此姿势多用于攻击对方下门。

图 3-9

9. 偷步（偷步）

它表示"偷一步"或"潜步向前"，准备发起攻击。此势既可踢击，也可变化为马步、丁步、弓步等其他姿势。

第一部分 中国武术的基础 17

图 3-10

10. 吊马（吊马）

它表示脚挂在马镫上。此姿势用于格挡扫腿、低踢、器械攻击等，常接踢腿。

七 星

图 3-11

当心对手的七个部位:

(1) 手　　　(2) 脚　　　(3) 肘

(4) 膝　　　(5) 肩　　　(6) 腿

(7) 头

三 盘

图 3-12

注意自身的三个前方：

（1）眼前　　（2）手前　　（3）腿前

第四章　腰部训练

腰部在功夫中有着重要地位。以下训练能够扩展腰部的活动范围，使其更加灵活。

图 4-1　前俯腰

（1）屈身以手触地；

（2）双脚总是绷直。

图 4-2　深俯腰

（1）屈身抱踝，以头贴膝；

（2）到后期，头应贴到小腿处，甚至能够到脚背。

图 4-3　侧俯腰

（1）下身不动，左转屈身；

（2）手掌触地；

（3）起身，向右重复同样的动作。

图 4-4　下腰

图 4-4A—图 4-4C 为下腰的具体步骤。

第一部分　中国武术的基础　21

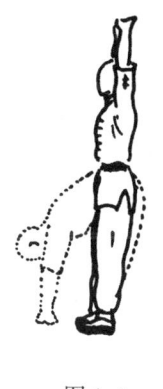

图 4-1

图 4-2

图 4-3

图 4-4A

图 4-4B

图 4-4C

图 4-5A

图 4-5B

图 4-5C

图4-5 转腰

（1）两脚并立，两手自然向上举起，身体转向左侧（图4-5A）；

（2）身体自左侧转向右侧（图4-5B）；

（3）右手呈钩状，左手随腰动，抓住右脚踝（图4-5C）；

（4）左手放开，身体从右向左重复刚才的动作。

图4-6 拧腰

（1）并步站立，右脚在左脚前交叉，身体转向右侧（图4-6A）；

（2）身体向后转，左脚碾地，右脚轻触地（图4-6B）；

（3）左转后，两膝略屈。

图4-7 翻腰

（1）如图4-7A，左脚在前蹲下，前胸贴前腿膝盖；

（2）身体转向右后方，两臂随身转动（图4-7B）；

（3）转腰后，右脚如图4-7B（虚线）所示在前；

（4）准备向左转。

第一部分　中国武术的基础　23

图 4-6A

图 4-6B

图 4-7A

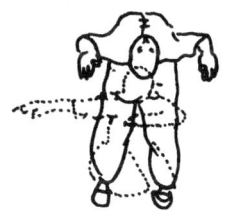

图 4-7B

第五章　腿部训练

踢击，特别是在北派功夫中，是最为重要的攻击方式。但是，应该警告人们滥用踢击的严重后果。确实腿比拳更具威力，攻击范围也更大，但是我们也必须注意到，当我们提腿踢击时就会影响整个身体的平衡。

我经常告诫我的学生："在训练时，能踢多高踢多高；但在实战中，则能踢多快踢多快。切记踢击勿高过腰带。"在我的门派中，踢击很少过腰，也从不用那些所谓的高踢或飞踢。腿部训练没有必要通过踢打坚硬的物体或沙包来增强力量，或使之坚硬，这在大多数武术流派中（不论南北）皆是如此。腿每天都支撑着我们的身体，本身已经极为有力，问题在于如何自然地训练它们。踢击训练包括聚力和发力，以及提升速度。

这里我介绍一些提升踢击能力的基本练习，其中第一部分着眼于拉伸韧带，扩展腿部的运动范围，第二部分则是关于如何自然地提升腿部力量。

第一部分　中国武术的基础　25

图 5-1

图 5-2

图 5-1　正压腿

如图 5-1 所示，将手放在右膝上以防止膝盖弯曲。勾脚下压，尽量以头触膝。每条腿做 15 下。

图 5-2　侧压腿

如图 5-2 所示，双手置于髋两侧。勾脚侧压，以头触脚。

图 5-3A

图 5-3B

图 5-3A—图 5-3B　吻靴

（1）下蹲，左脚伸直，勾脚尖，脚跟触地；

（2）两手握住左脚往回拉，身体前屈，亲吻鞋子。左右交换练习。

图 5-4A   图 5-4B

注意：刚开始练习时，先以头触膝，再慢慢往前够。

图 5-4A—图 5-4B 卧靴

与前一姿势相同，但这次前屈时尽量以头触脚，身体右侧贴着左脚。重复12—20次后，换右脚。

图 5-5—图 5-6

图 5-5 和图 5-6 是难度更高的腿部训练。

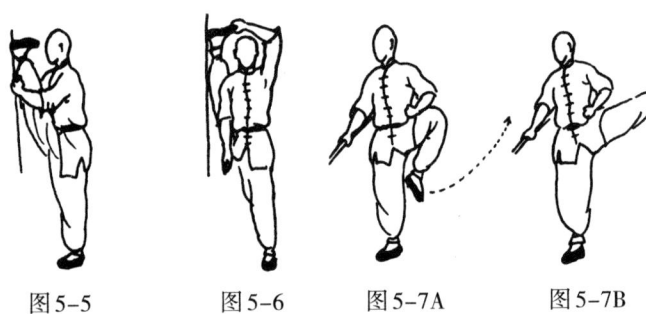

图 5-5   图 5-6   图 5-7A   图 5-7B

图 5-7A—图 5-7B 侧控腿

在中国功夫中这一训练叫做吊腿。当腿抬到既定高度，必须悬在那，能吊多久就吊多久。

（1）如图5-7A所示，右手扶杠；

（2）勾脚尖，慢慢提起左脚，与地面约成90°，悬在那里保持一会儿；

（3）放下，再重复同样的步骤。

图5-8A—图5-8B　前控腿

（1）与前姿势相同；

（2）但这次不是控抬腿，而是勾脚尖，将腿向前缓缓举起，直到腿与地面至少呈90°角；

（3）维持这个姿势一会儿，然后再重复。

图5-8A　　　　　图5-8B　　　　　图5-9

图5-9

这种前高踢仅在练习时用。

（1）两手握拳置于髋两侧，右脚向前迈出一步，左脚在后；

（2）左脚勾着脚尖，绷直向上踢击，目标是假想敌的头部；

（3）左脚放下与右脚平行，再向前迈一步，右脚在后，准备踢击。

注意：

（1）踢击时，注意别弯腰，腰部不要过于前倾；

（2）身体切勿后倒；

（3）支撑脚须牢牢抓住地面。

图5-10 斜挂

（1）与图5-9姿势相同，但左腿朝右耳侧面踢；

（2）两手侧平举以保持身体平衡。

图5-11 侧踢

（1）身体立正，右脚略微朝右迈出，身体如图5-11所示转向右侧；

图5-10

图5-11

（2）左脚朝左耳际踢起；

（3）左脚落地时略微向左侧迈出（脚尖外展），身体转向左侧；

（4）按同样的方法踢击。

图5-12—图5-14

（1）图5-12和图5-14是外摆腿和里合腿的练习姿势。左右脚重复练习；

（2）图5-13是摆腿时的正确姿势。

图5-15—图5-17

这些都是用于实战的踢击。这里我只介绍功夫中的三个基本踢法：侧撑腿、前蹬腿和直挑腿。

图5-15 撑腿

（1）如图5-15所示，身体站直；

（2）迈右步，左脚如鞭子一般，集中全身力量踢出；

（3）快速收回左脚，落于右脚前；

（4）右脚也以同样的方式踢击。

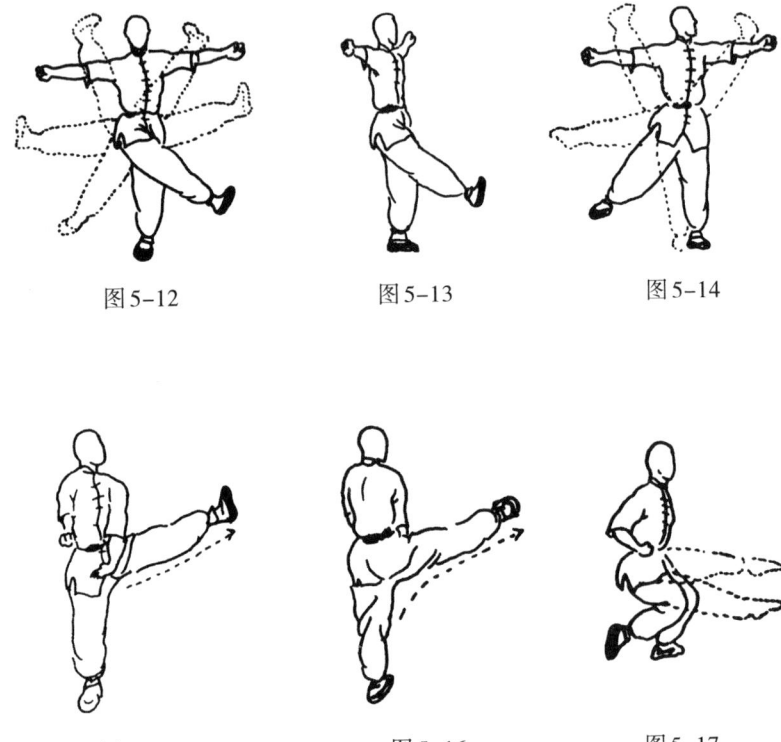

图 5-12　　　　　图 5-13　　　　　图 5-14

图 5-15　　　　　图 5-16　　　　　图 5-17

第六章　功夫中的阴阳哲理

　　由于此书只论及基本的功夫技巧，起初我并不打算将此节纳入其中。但转念一想，我相信读者会从中国哲学的阴阳理念中获益良多。不管哪一个格斗术派别的练习者，他的技术都极有可能从中得到提高。

　　武术的基本结构来源于阴阳学说。在"阴阳"的观念里，宇宙中存在着一对相伴相生、处于永不停歇的运动之中的力量。这一中国哲学的理念可以套用在任何事物上，但在这里我们只讨论它与中国功夫的关系。上图圆中的黑色部分叫"阴"，"阴"可以指代世间任何否定的、消极的、柔和的、虚幻的事物，如女性、月亮、黑暗等。

圆中与"阴"相对的另一半是"阳",它象征肯定的、积极的、刚强的、现实的事物,如男性、太阳、光明、白昼等。

大多数人错误地认为阴阳图,即太极,是二元对立的,即"阳"是"阴"的反面,反之亦然。但如果我们将一个整体一分为二,我们将无法领悟到真谛。事实上,任何事物都有其互补的一面,只是在人们的思维和认识中它们才被分割成相互对立的。太阳并非月亮的反面,因为它们相伴相生,我们离开其中任何一方都无法生存。同样,男人和女人也是相互依存的;如果没有男人,我们如何知道有"女人"这个概念?反过来也一样。因此,阴阳的统一性在生活中是必须的。如果一个人骑车去一个地方,他不能同时踩两个踏板或者两个都不踩。为了前进,他必须踩一个的同时松开另一个。因此,车的前进需要"踩"和"放"的统一。踩是放的结果,反之亦然。

在阴阳图里,黑色的部分中有个白点,白色的部分里有个黑点。这可以用来解释生活中的平衡,因为没有任何事物在走向任一极端时能够持久,不管是消极的还是积极的。因此,刚中寓柔,柔中寓刚,这就是为何习武之人需要像弹簧般柔韧。注意,树刚易折,而竹子随风弯曲,因此弯而不折。因而在功夫,或其他武术体系中,习武者需柔而不软,刚而不僵;即使他再强壮,也需习以柔性以进行防御。如果刚中无柔,则非真刚;同样,如果柔中带刚,则没有人能突破他的防守。这一中庸原则是保护自己的最佳方法。只有当我们接受了在任何事物中都存在着阴阳合一,而不将其对立,我们才能在超然和平衡中拥有一份宁静。即使我们走向消极或积极中的任一极端,我们也可以顺势掌控自身。顺应,而非死守,乃是避免极端的真正方法。

当阴阳运动走向一个极端,反作用力就开始起作用。阳极则阴,阴随阳动,阴极则阳,二者互为因果。例如,一个人拼命工作到极限就会疲乏,需要休息(由阳至阴),休息后方可再战(由阴至阳)。这一阴阳转换持续不断,永不停歇。阴阳理论在功夫理论中的应用就是顺势而为,即必须顺应对手的力,而非以力抵力。试想A向B发力攻击,B不应与其硬性相抗或完全躲避——这是B能够做出的两个对立的极端反应。取而代之的是,B应以很小的力去促成A的攻击,以自身的运动引导A的力量——如同屠夫为了保存屠刀,沿着骨头而非向着骨头进行切割。习武之人为保护自己,也应顺应对手的力,不要抵抗甚至与之搏斗（而应是无为的——自发的、本能的动作）。对 A 的力量的顺引将把 A 的力量返回到其自身，以将他打败。

当习武之人最终明白了阴阳理论，他就不再为那些所谓的"柔"和"刚"瞎忙活了，他只是顺势而为。事实上，所有那些传统的条条框框和限定技术都将被抛之脑后，他的动作源于日常。他无需像众多大师一样用意念或内力来证明自己；对他来说，长期的武术练习终会返璞归真，只有那些"半吊子"才需证明和吹捧自己。

第二部分
中国功夫的技术

第七章　中国拳法的实例

图 7-1A

图 7-1B

图 7-1C

图 7-1A　A 以左弓步冲拳。①

图 7-1B　B 转腰，右手向上拨开 A 的攻击。与其他武术流派以强对强、阻挡进攻不同，中国功夫倾向于化解对方的攻击并将其力反作用到对方身上。（注意：图中白色箭头表示腰部转动的方向。）

图 7-1C　接着，B 顺势以标指戳对方眼。留意另一手处于防守中。（注意：多次练习后，阻挡和攻击应一气呵成。）

---

① 攻击方 A 为木村武之（Taky Kimura）。——译者注

图 7-2A

图 7-2B

图 7-2C

图 7-2A　A 以左冲拳先发起进攻。

图 7-2B　B 上步呈中式,以左拍手化解对方来拳的同时,直接以右插捶攻击对方。

图 7-2C　A 猛出右拳进攻。B 维持站姿,以左手阻挡攻击,同时右手翻掌卜插对方喉部(右插喉掌)。

图7-3A

图7-3A　A以右冲拳先发起进攻。

图 7-3B

图 7-3B　觉察 A 的攻击后，B 立即向后退，拍挡其来拳的同时，以右侧撑腿踢击对手。（注意：B 的右手必须放在攻击位置上。）

图7-4A

图7-4B

图7-4C

图7-4A　A以右钩拳进攻。

图7-4B　B侧闪转腰，格挡攻击的同时，以标指戳对方的眼睛。

图7-4C　A再次攻击，以左上钩拳攻击B的上腹部。B侧闪，同时右手下拦封住对方的拳头，左掌以标指再次插对方眼。

图7-5A

图7-5B

图 7-5C

图 7-5A　A 抓住 B 的双手。

图 7-5B　B 右脚向前一步，同时右手拍击对方右手，使其左手拇指与右手腕骨相撞。

图 7-5C　当 A 松手后，B 以左冲拳垂直打击对方面门。

图 7-6A

图 7-6B

图 7-6C

图 7-6A　　　　　　A 从后熊抱 B。B 放松，重心下沉。

图 7-6B、图 7-6C　B 转腰，以肘击 A，同时狠踩 A 的脚。

图7-7A

图7-7A　A呈左弓步,以右冲拳进攻。

图 7-7B

图 7-7B　B 侧闪，化解攻击，并以插捶击打 A 的肋骨。

图7-8A

图7-8A　A以右侧撑腿进攻。

第二部分 中国功夫的技术 53

图 7-8B

图 7-8B　B以右钩手下拨（注意左手处于防守之中），同时以直挑腿踢击对方裆部。

图 7-9A

图 7-9B

图 7-9C

图 7-9A　A 推 B。

图 7-9B　B 转腰，如图所示向前一步拨开 A 的攻击，并以插捶攻击。

图 7-9C　B 翻右手牵引 A，快速突入并以膝进攻 A。

图 7-10A

图 7-10B

图7-10C

图7-10A、图7-10B　A猛扑过来,以右冲拳攻击。[1]

图7-10C　　　　　　B不后退,转腰朝对手进攻方向顺引对方力量。

---

[1] 攻击方A为杰西·格洛弗（Jesse Glover）。——译者注

图7-10D

图7-10D　A试图抽出他的右拳,以左手猛攻。

第二部分 中国功夫的技术 59

图 7-10E

图 7-10E 顺着 A 右拳的收势,B 左手下压封锁 A 的双手,同时以右冲捶进攻 A。

图 7-11A

图 7-11B

第二部分 中国功夫的技术 61

图7-11C

图7-11A、7-11B　如图所示,A试图将B翻摔。(功夫中有36式摔技和72式关节锁定技)

图7-11C　　　　B转腰,抓住A的左手,同时扭转右肩并以其下压A的肩膀。

图7-11D

图7-11D　B右脚猛地后踢呈弓步,将A摔出。

图 7-11E

图 7-11E　再接以一记膝击或拳击，彻底击倒对手。

图7-12A

图7-12A A突入,以右标指进攻。

图7-12B

图7-12B　B不后退，而是转腰顺引A的力量，同时以掌骨击打对方。[①]

[①] 防守方B为查理斯·吴先生是柔道黑带2段。——译者注

图7-13A

图7-13A A以右冲拳攻击。B以右手拨开进攻。(注意:左手处于防守状态。)

图7-13B

图7-13B　A撤回右手,快速出左拳攻击B的上腹部。B仅以左手向下拍击A拳,右手则从先前位置直戳A的眼睛。

图7-14A

图7-14A　A以左拳进攻。B以右钩手拨开A的进攻。

图7-14B

图7-14B　A撤回左手，疾出右拳。B左手拨开其来拳，顺其收势，右手从先前的钩手变插捶攻击。

图 7-15A

图 7-15A　此时此刻，X并不将注意力集中于任何一个人的举动。他只需静待其变，不去想随后的结果或其他东西。①

---

① 攻击方B为詹姆斯·德迈尔。——译者注

图7-15B

图7-15B　A以右钩拳攻击X。X转身阻挡,以右标指直
戳A(注意步法的变化)。

图7-15C

图7-15B、图7-15C 在X使A无力化的同时，B以右冲拳进攻。X转腰拨开攻击，以右撑腿侧踢B。

图 7–15D

图 7–15C、图 7–15D　此时，C 以右冲拳突入，攻击 X 的面门。X 拨开拳，同时以插捶反击。

74　李小龙基本中国拳法

图7-16A

图7-16B

图 7-16C

图 7-16A、图 7-16B　A 突入，以右冲拳直攻心窝。X 拨开来拳，以挂捶击打 A 的太阳穴进行反击。此时，B 趁势闯进。

图 7-16B、图 7-16C　X 回以左扫拳，如图所示以跪马闪进，攻击 B 的裆部。

图7-17A

图7-17A　A以插捶直击B的心口。

图 7-17B

图 7-17B　B转腰，钩住A的拳头，以插捶回击。

图 7-18A

图 7-18A　A和B均以预备姿势站好。

图7-18B

图7-18B　A以指戳B的咽喉。B以转腰牵引A的力量化解攻击。这个进攻的化解不是靠手而是靠腰的转动,以真正使对方失去平衡。

图 7-19A

图 7-19B

第二部分 中国功夫的技术 81

图 7-19C

图 7-19A　A、B 双方正常站立，A 向 B 的手施加压力。

图 7-19B　B 朝 A 施力方向猛拉 A，同时垫步向前蹬踢（注意左手放于防护位置）。

图 7-19C　A 以左手阻挡 B 的前蹬。B 顺势转腰低位侧踢 A 的膝盖。

第八章　不同的功夫风格

上乘的功夫建立在简洁的基础上。只有那些不成熟的武术体系才充满多余的动作。

简洁是长期深入研究人体运动方式的自然结果。好的武术家是简单主义者。

下面展示的是较慢的武术体系与更为有效的功夫相对抗的例子。

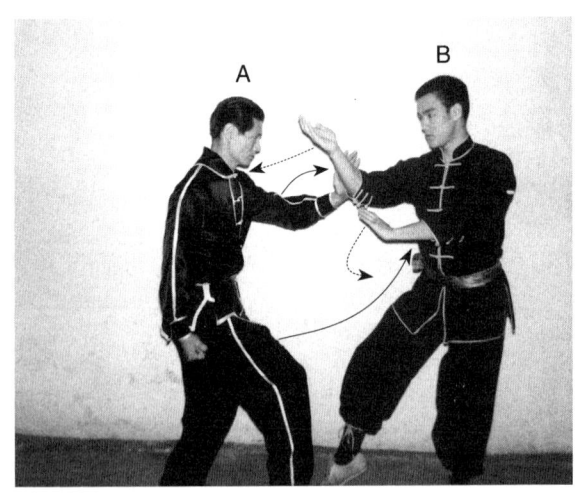

图8-1A

图 8-1B

图 8-1A　A以炮捶进攻。①

图 8-1B　B没有多余的动作，仅下钩手阻挡A的攻击，趁A的力量往回收时，顺势砍向A的颈动脉。

---

① 攻击方A为严镜海。——译者注

图 8-2A

图 8-2B

第二部分 中国功夫的技术 85

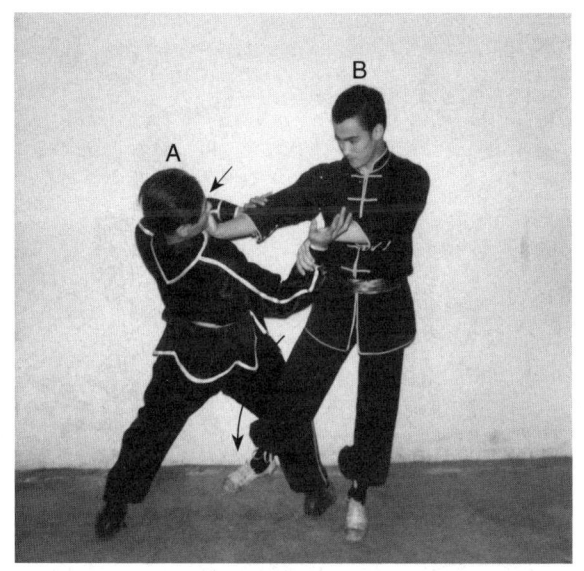

图 8-2C

图 8-2A　　　　　在功夫中，没有人会像图 8-2A 中 B 一样抓着对方。为了举例说明，我们假设 B 抓着 A 的衣服。

图 8-2A、图 8-2B　A 右脚向前一步，企图以右肘向上攻击。但在远距离攻击中，使用肘击是危险的；如你所见，A 攻击时，B 只需出直拳反击（图 8-2B）。肘应在近身搏斗中使用。

图 8-2C　　　　　B 继续进攻，使用交叉绊摔将 A 摔出，同时以掌跟击打 A 的下巴。

图8-3A

图8-3A 被某人抓住时,比起实施关节技或推开对方,直接踢对方的胫骨更为有效。如果对方另一只手没抓住你,直接出拳进攻他。我们假设B抓住A的手,A右脚迈进一步,同时朝B的方向推B的肘,试图破坏B的平衡。

图 8-3B

图 8-3B　在此过程中，B 可在 A 向前一步时踢击其裆部，或者戳 A 的眼睛。或者如图 8-3B 所示，B 可以同时以标指和直挑腿进攻。

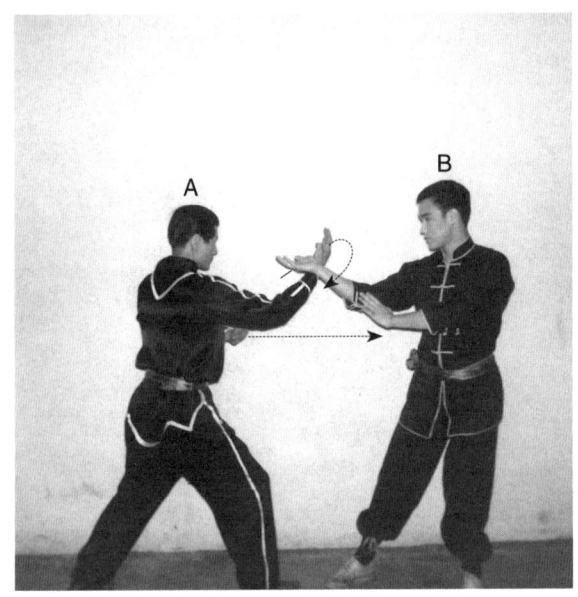

图 8-4A

图 8-4A　A 抓着 B 的手往回拉，企图以左肘进攻 B 的肋骨。

图 8-4B

图 8-4B　B沉肘,顺势左转面向对手,同时以左指直戳A,也可以追加直踢。

图 8-5A

图 8-5B

第二部分 中国功夫的技术 91

图 8-5C

图 8-5A B 以右冲捶进攻,A 以扭马拨开 B 的拳头。

图 8-5B A 向前一步,在 B 身体稍右侧呈马步,准备以切掌侧击 B 的肋骨。而实际上,B 此时既可以用指直戳,也可以用左掌边缘击打拦截 A 的肘部。

图 8-5C 当 A 突入时,B 在相同位置上用右手拨开 A 的进攻,同时以右钩踢反击。

第九章　还原与见证：
李小龙武术习练及照片

　　将随后的图片和注解作为本书的补充部分，是艰难考虑之后所作的决定。因为显而易见的是，这些照片原本并非为此书所拍摄，而我们也对其由来和意图知之甚少。

　　如果家父希望将这些照片作为本书的修订版或其他书中的一部分，那么他一定会去做。他在拍这些照片并附上注解时，脑中似乎确实在构思着一本书。但他是否已完成了这本新书的照片和文本，或其创作发展是否完全背离了这一部分内容的理念，我们永远无法得知。

　　正如家母在本书前言中提到的那样，随着家父武术理念的发展，他最终改变了《李小龙基本中国拳法》再版的想法。但时间证明，李小龙的功夫和他的武术知识一直吸引着武术界。正是出于这个原因，我们不仅决定再版《李小龙基本中国拳法》，还决定加入更多的资料以更好地呈现家父的武术知识基础及其演变。

这部分的照片和注解并不构成一个完整的章节,甚至不构成一个完整的主题。然而,这批照片和注释包含着李小龙武术人生的历程。之所以将它们原模原样地展示给读者,是因为我们和编辑都不想对它们进行任何解释。我们希望读者能像我们一样发现这几页内容的趣味,能花时间翻阅它们,并以全面的眼光看待照片中的武术。在满怀教学热情的同时,家父也是一个技艺高超的学生。别的不说,这部分内容就是一个对武术满怀热情并愿意同他人分享的男人的见证。

李香凝

2008年

图 A-1

图 A-1　A、B 以准备姿势面对面站好。

编者按：本部分图片的编号保留了李小龙手稿中的排列顺序。

图 A-2

图 A-2 在第一个动作中，A 封阻 B 的右手，同时击打 B 的咽喉（注意封锁 B 的脚防止其踢击）。

图 A-3

图 A-3　B 拍开 A 的右手化解其攻击。

第二部分　中国功夫的技术　97

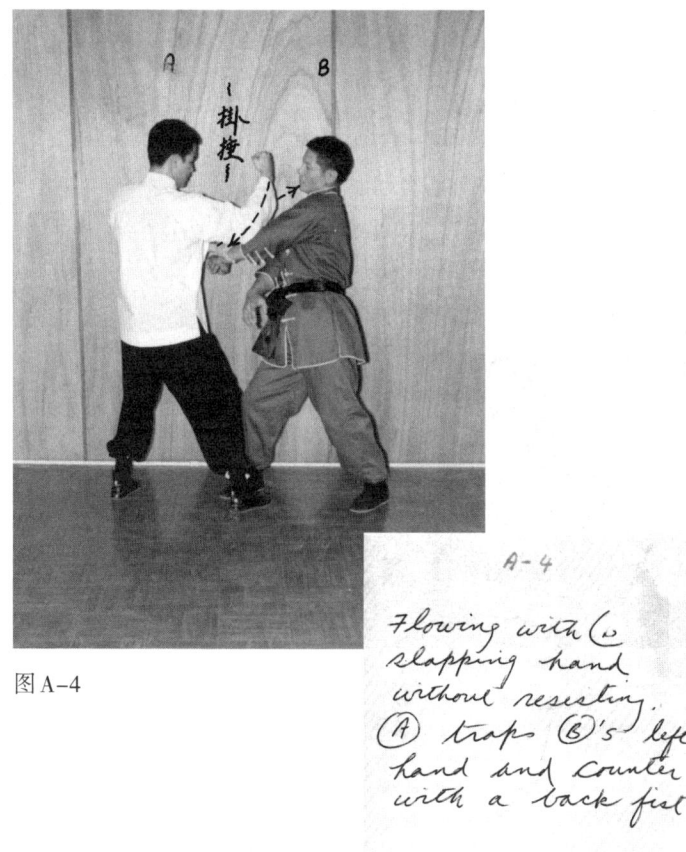

图 A-4

图 A-4　A不顶不抗，顺势被拍掉右手，同时搂抓B的左手并顺势以挂捶反击。

图 A-5

A-5

Closing in, A comes in with two straight punches as shown in the following two pictures. [observe how B is "locked" without any striking or kicking room]

第二部分　中国功夫的技术　99

图 A-6

图 A-5、图 A-6　A 拉近与 B 的距离，如图所示以两个直拳进攻（注意 B 是如何被封锁到没有攻击和踢击的余地）。

图 B-1

图 B-1　A以冲捶直击B的面部。

第二部分 中国功夫的技术 101

图 B-2

B-2

Advancing, B deflects A's punch and strike him simultaneously by turning his waist. The deflection should be outward and upward without over-reaching, thus going off the body.

图 B-2　B 由下向上、由内向外拨开 A 来拳的同时，转腰进攻。左手拨拳不宜离身体太远。

图 B-3

图 B-3　A试图以右直踢进攻。B拉近距离，挡住脚踢，同时用进攻的右手抓向A的眼睛。所有的动作都在B感觉到猛拉和A右肩右手放松的一瞬间完成。

图 C-1

图 C-1 这是一个传统的功夫动作。A 以弓式冲拳进攻。B 以右前臂阻挡。①

---

① 图中 A 为严镜海，B 为李鸿新。——译者注

图 C-2

图 C-2　A 挑腿冲拳。B 截断其攻击。

图 C-3

图 C-3 在右脚落地呈马步前，A 突进，以拳直击 B 的上腹部。（注意：A 的左手处于防守中，同时右脚锁住了 B 的右脚防止其踢击。）B 如图所示挡住了 A 的拳头。

图 C-4

图 C-4　顺着 B 左手下挂，A 拍击 B 的右肘并以右挂捶反击（动作一气呵成）。注意 A 缩短了距离，并以右脚封锁了 B 的右脚。

第二部分　中国功夫的技术　　107

图 D

图 D　在对手企图使对方偏离中心线时，可用标指。标指也可被成功用来对付对手的佯攻或抡臂出拳。这是简单实用的技术，你会为如此简单的动作竟然能阻断并打乱对手花哨的动作而感到惊奇。

图 E-1

编者按：由于李小龙先生并未对图 E-1 至图 E-6 作注释，我们在此保留原样。

图 E-2

图 E-3

第二部分　中国功夫的技术　　111

图 E-4

图 E-5

第二部分　中国功夫的技术　　113

图 E-6

图 F-1

图 F-1 以下图片拍摄于对旧金山拉尔夫·卡斯特罗肯波空手道工作室的一次访问中。此图中李小龙（左）和埃德·帕克以摆桩，即预备式站好。

图 F-2

图 F-2 从左至右：李小龙、埃德·帕克、严镜海、拉尔夫·卡斯特罗。

编者按：埃德·帕克和拉尔夫·卡斯特罗都是肯波流空手道的黑带教练。

图F-3

图F-3 从左至右：在畅谈功夫的本书作者李小龙、埃德·帕克和严镜海。

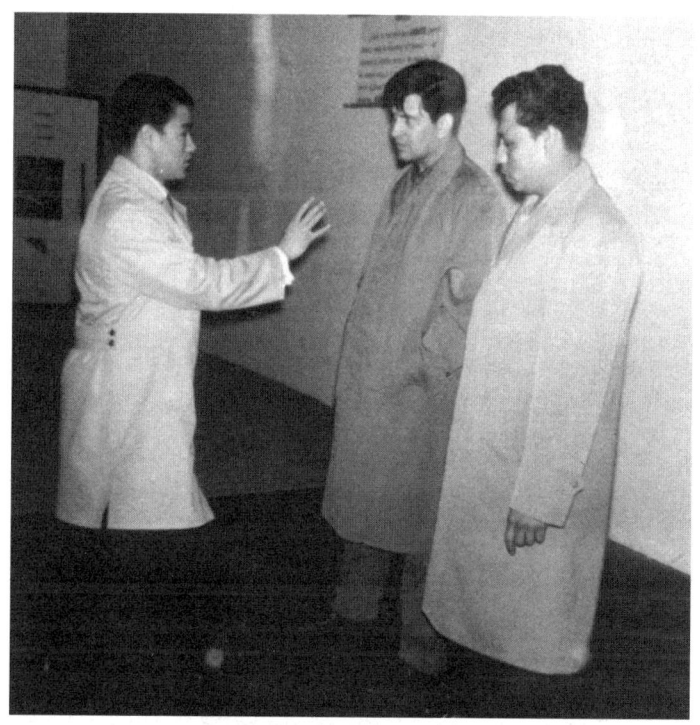

图 F-4

图 F-4　从左至右：李小龙和埃德·帕克、拉尔夫·卡斯特罗在卡斯特罗宽敞的工作室中。

附 录
回忆李小龙

希望与荣耀：李小龙的自卫术

正如我之前在《唐手功夫》（Modern Kung Fu Karate）一书中提到的那样，劈砖和铁砂掌的练习并非功夫训练的必要部分。此书所谈到的内容则全部用以自卫。

我很高兴李小龙先生能够答应出版此书，这是他的"中国拳法系列丛书"中的第一本，比敝人的拙作更开阔完善。

李小龙先生三年前从中国来美，是当今美国最具权威的中国拳师之一。他自小师从多名武师学习中国南北武术。在13岁那年，他遇到了咏春拳宗师叶问，自此潜心研习咏春拳法。经过多年的训练和频繁的实战，他成为叶问门下获准教拳的弟子中最年轻的一位。

赴美之后，李小龙精心挑选了几名弟子，潜心教授功夫。在其追随者中有柔道和空手道黑带、其他武术流派的弟子、拳击手等。

除通晓各派拳术之外，李小龙亦深谙道家学说和禅学理念。他曾在美国一部有关东方哲学和功夫的电视剧中担任指导工作。

李小龙先生想通过他诚挚的努力，将中国自卫术的真实面目展现给世人，这也使他成为因中国功夫这一古老而高雅的艺术赢得荣誉的人。

在与李小龙先生的多次友好切磋中，我深受震撼。即使他蒙着眼，一旦他黏住我的手，我便无法近身或施展拳脚。

我深信这本书不仅能使美国人对自卫术原理有更好的了解，其他东方武学的练习者也会深受其益。本书通过清晰的插图，清楚讲解了掌握各个技巧的所有步骤。

奥斯卡·王尔德曾说过："模仿是最诚挚的赞美。"若果真如此，那么我对李小龙先生最诚挚的赞美就是以他的方法去改善我所有的功夫。当他向我展示了他那基于内在能量的攻击方法时，我发现它比我先前练习的铁砂掌更加有力。他的功夫的优越性就在于精炼和高效，远胜于我过往多年所学。他的攻击力量来自于腰部和意念，因此我现在一直主张碎砖并不能真正检验力量。

不论何时，只要我俩有机会一起训练，我都感到受益匪浅。

现在，李小龙先生正通过著书、上电视向来自不同种族、宗教、民族的人传授功夫——这正逐渐成为未来功夫教练的核心事务，以防止功夫这一古老的中国技艺发生滥用和商业化。

我完全同意李先生所言："当越来越多的美国人学习到真正的中国功夫时，将会有越来越少的人还敢去冒充功夫'行家'。"

严镜海

编者按：严镜海先生步入武术殿堂是从研习柔术和少林拳法开始的。认识李小龙后，他成为李小龙的学生，并担任奥克兰截拳道学校的助理教练。他们保持着独特的关系，不仅是忘年交，还是彼此在武术和哲学上的老师。严镜海先生留给后人的财富中也包括他有关现代武术训练的系列丛书。

功夫天才李小龙

这仅是我观察李小龙所得的总体印象。

他的功夫体系独特、精准,且极为实用。其原理和理念合乎逻辑,近乎完美;其道理简单又深奥;其动作粘黏连随、柔中带刚、虚实结合、阴阳合一、方中有圆;此外,李小龙那不可思议的速度和爆发力也让人称奇。

他不仅精通自身拳法,同时风趣健谈。他对于其他中国武艺及其历史背景和哲学底蕴知之甚详,其讲解使人无法不尽心倾听。

他是我见过的少有的天赋异禀的人,而他也毫无疑问地在武艺方面发挥着这一天赋。

得知他在写有关功夫的书籍,我很高兴。他坚定了我对功夫的信心,同时他也将极大地弘扬纯正的中国功夫。

埃德·帕克

编者按：埃德·帕克先生是加利福尼亚州帕萨迪纳市著名的肯波流空手道黑带教练，也是国际肯波流空手道协会的主席和创始人，著有《肯波流》一书。他以"美国空手道之父"的称号享誉世界，是美国肯波流空手道的开山鼻祖。

别开生面的中国搏击术

我强烈推荐李小龙的这本关于中国功夫的书籍。这本书信息丰富,展示了杰出的中国自卫方式。我曾看过作者的教学,我认为它们简练又有效。我为这位年轻的中国拳师所具有的广博知识感到惊讶。

他的咏春拳和我以往见过的任何武术都不同,我从未见过类似的功夫。

我坚信,如果我重新开始练武,这将是我要学习的武术。

李小龙师父是一位绅士,但他居然能把他那绅士般的武术技法用于实战。

我曾见他出手,似黑豹般优雅敏捷,又如闪电般迅速。在中国搏击术中,他堪称大师。

威利·杰伊

编者按：杰伊教授是小循环柔术的创始人和顶级大师，柔术黑带10段，柔道黑带6段。他是加利福尼亚州阿拉梅达"艾兰德柔道柔术俱乐部"的总教练、柔术黑带5段，讲道馆柔道黑带3段。

基本中國拳法

（英文版）

FOREWORD
By Linda Lee Cadwell

Chinese Gung Fu: The Philosophical Art of Self-Defense was the first and only book Bruce Lee published about Chinese martial arts before his untimely death in 1973. The book represents a sampling of the knowledge Bruce accumulated from the time he began martial arts training as a boy in Hong Kong up to his first five years in the United States. Under Master Yip Man, Bruce studied the traditional Gung Fu style of Wing Chung, but through his study and personal experience with other practitioners, he also knew a great deal about other styles of Gung Fu. He kept copious notes, clippings and hand drawings of various styles and weaponry, both ancient and modern. Some of these are referred to in this small book.

In the years following the publication of *Chinese Gung Fu: The Philosophical Art of Self-Defense*, Bruce's direction in martial arts development veered away from the traditional styles toward the evolution of his own martial way that he called Jeet Kune Do, or "The Way of the Intercepting Fist." In fact, so great was his need to liberate himself from classical martial arts in later years, he asked the publishers to cease production of this book.

Chinese Gung Fu: The Philosophical Art of Self-Defense was republished after Bruce's passing and continues to be published today because it has come to be considered a classic, as well as a legitimate resource, on Chinese Gung Fu styles and techniques. The book also demonstrates Bruce's fundamental background in Gung Fu and is a historical snapshot into the life of the legendary Bruce Lee.

L. L. Cadwell
2008

DEDICATION

To my parents –

Mr. and Mrs. Lee Hoi Chuen

and to my very good friend –

Mrs. Eva Tso

– B. Lee

CONTENTS

Foreword by Linda Lee Cadwell v

About the Author by James Y. Lee 1

About the Author by Ed Parker 4

About the Author by Wally Jay 5

Introduction by Bruce Lee 6

PART 1: CHINESE MARTIAL ART 11
    Several Important Pointers 15
    Gung Fu Stances 16
    The Seven Stars 26
    The Three Fronts 27
    On Waist Training 28
    On Leg Training 32
    The Basic Theory of Yin and Yang 38

PART 2: CHINESE GUNG FU TECHNIQUES 43
    Difference in Gung Fu Styles 88

PART 3: ADDITIONAL TECHNIQUES 99
    Introduction by Shannon Lee 100
    Additional Pictures 122

– All drawings by Bruce Lee –

ABOUT THE AUTHOR
By James Y. Lee

As mentioned before in my previous book—*Modern Kung Fu Karate*—that the Brick Breaking and Iron Hand Training are not a necessary part of Gung Fu training, this book deals strictly with self-defense.

Unlike my previous books on Gung Fu, written by one of limited knowledge, I was very happy when Mr. Bruce Lee was persuaded to come out with this, his first of a series of books on the ancient art of Gung Fu.

Bruce Lee, one of the highest authorities in the Chinese art of Gung Fu in the United States today, came from China three years ago. At an early age, Mr. Lee started Gung Fu training from various instructors from both Northern and Southern schools of Gung Fu. At thirteen, he met Master Yip Man, leader of the Wing Chung School of Gung Fu, and since then he has devoted himself to that system. After years of daily training and engagements in competitive matches, he was awarded the rank of instructor—the youngest to achieve it in that school.

Since his arrival in the United States, Mr. Lee has selected a few disciplines and devoted his time to teaching them. Among his many followers are Judo and Karate black belt holders, Gung Fu students of other systems, boxers, etc.

Aside from his knowledge of the various schools of Gung Fu, Mr. Lee is also well versed in Taoism and Ch'an (Zen). He has conducted a T.V. series in the U.S. on Oriental philosophy and Gung Fu.

Mr. Lee will be one who will bring credit to the ancient and noble art of Chinese Gung Fu by his sincere effort to present a true perspective of the art of Chinese self-defense.

I was really impressed when in friendly sparring matches with Mr. Bruce Lee, I couldn't penetrate or land a telling blow or kick—even when he was blindfolded—once his hands were "sticking" to mine.

I am sure this book will bring to the citizens of the U.S. a better understanding of the principles that make Gung Fu such an effective system in defense. Students of other Oriental systems will benefit greatly from this book. In well-illustrated photos, it clearly explains all the steps to master the various techniques.

Oscar Wilde once said, "Imitation is the most sincere compliment." If so, I have paid Mr. Bruce Lee a sincere compliment by changing all my Gung Fu techniques to his methods. When he demonstrated his type of striking, which is based on inner energy, I found it much more powerful than the power I had developed from previous Iron Hand Training. The superiority of his Gung Fu is more refined and effective than that which I have learned in all my past years. Since his striking power is generated from the waist and mind, I have always maintained that the power to break bricks is not the true test of actual application of energy in real combat.

I always benefit greatly whenever we get a chance to train together.

At present Mr. Lee—through his books, T.V. appearances and Gung Fu instructions to Americans, regardless of race, creed or national origin—is in the process of developing a nucleus of future Gung Fu instructors to keep the ancient Chinese art from being exploited and commercialized as evidenced, unfortunately, in some other Oriental systems.

I am in complete accord with the author when he says, "When more and more Americans are instructed in the authentic techniques of Gung Fu, less and less people will be able to pass themselves off as self-styled Gung Fu 'experts.'"

J.Y. Lee

Publisher's Note: Mr. James Lee began his martial arts training in Jujitsu and Sil Lum Gung Fu. Upon meeting Bruce Lee, he became a student of Mr. Lee's art and then an assistant instructor at the Oakland Jeet Kune Do School. They had a unique chemistry that bonded them as lifelong friends as well as perpetual students of the martial arts and philosophy. Mr. James Lee's legacy includes a series of books on modern Gung Fu training.

ABOUT THE AUTHOR
By Ed Parker

This is just a summation of my impressions as I observed Bruce Lee.

His system is unique, precise and extremely practical. Its principles and concepts are logical and basically sound. It is based on simplicity, but yet it is intricate; the movements are sticky but yet slippery, soft but yet firm, obvious but yet deceptive, dual but yet having oneness, angular but yet circular, not to mention the incredible speed and snap executed by Bruce Lee.

Not only is he highly adept in his system, but as a conversationalist he is very interesting. His descriptive knowledge of other Chinese systems and their historical and philosophical background cannot help but make one an attentive listener.

He is one of the very few that I have seen who is gifted with a natural ability, a gift which he undoubtedly has put to work (as evidenced by his superb skill).

I am glad to learn that he is writing books on Gung Fu. He confirms my faith in Gung Fu and will be a great stimulant in presenting the art of Gung Fu in its true and authentic light.

E. Parker

Publisher's Note: Mr. Ed Parker was the well-known black belt Kenpo Karate instructor of Pasadena, California, president and founder of the International Kenpo Karate Association and author of *Kenpo*. He was known worldwide as "Mr. Karate" and is considered the founder of American Kenpo.

ABOUT THE AUTHOR
By Wally Jay

I highly recommend Mr. Bruce Lee's book on the Chinese art of Gung Fu. This informative book will reveal an outstanding style of Chinese self-defense. I have witnessed the teaching methods of the author and I find them concise and effective. I was also astonished with the vast knowledge this youthful Chinese master possesses.

His Wing Chung system is unlike any other system of Gung Fu that I have seen. I have never seen anything like it.

I am convinced that this would be the system I would study if I were to begin my Gung Fu training again.

Master Bruce Lee, who is a gentleman, can actually apply his seemingly gentle method in actual application.

I have seen him perform with the grace and agility of a panther and with lighting speed. He is truly a master of a great style of Chinese fighting.

W. Jay

Publisher's Note: Professor Jay, founder and great grandmaster of Professor Jay's Small Circle Jujitsu, holds a 10th degree black belt in Jujitsu and a 6th degree black belt in Judo. At the time of the original writing of his introduction, he was the head instructor of the Island Judo and Jujitsu Club in Alameda, California, and he was a 5th degree black belt in Jujitsu and a 3rd degree black belt in Kodokan Judo.

INTRODUCTION

The center of the Far Eastern martial arts has been the art of Gung Fu, whose principles and techniques pervaded and influenced the different arts of Oriental self-defense. Because Gung Fu has been shrouded under a veil of utmost secrecy, it is very seldom heard of in the Western world as well as many other Far Eastern countries.

Its history covers four thousand years. At first in the midst of antiquity, Gung Fu was simply a no-holds-barred type of fighting, but as the centuries went by, countless generations of its practitioners gradually perfected it, smoothing out the rough spots and polishing the techniques, until it began to emerge as something definitely superior. Later on, the studies of anatomy, religion and psychology were included, and Gung Fu advanced one more step to a highly scientific and philosophical type of self-defense. That was around two or three thousand years ago! Gung Fu is for health promotion, cultivation of mind and self-protection. Its philosophy is based on the integral parts of the philosophies of Taoism (道 學), Ch'an (Zen 禪) and I'Ching (Book of Changes 易 經)—the ideal of giving with adversity, to bend slightly and spring back stronger than before, and to adapt oneself harmoniously to the opponent's movements without striving or resisting. The techniques of Gung Fu emphasize not power but conservation of energy and moderation without going to either extreme (Yin and Yang 陰 陽). That is why a true Gung Fu man never opposes forces (which will create reaction) or gives way completely; he is simply pliable as a spring. He seeks to merge harmoniously <u>with</u>

the oncoming force of the opponent—to be the complement and not the opposite of the opponent's force.

It has been quite a number of years that I have indulged myself in Wing Chung, the School of Artlessness; my mind is no longer distracted by the opponent, "self," or formal techniques, etc. I have made my opponent's techniques my techniques; my task is simply to complete the other half of the "oneness," and my action is that of Wu-Wei (spontaneous act), which is according to the circumstances without pre-arrangement. The training of mind and imagination, imagination and Ch'i (breath), breath and energy, etc., are all gone. There is nothing to <u>try</u> to do; everything simply flows.

Now I am asked, by a very good friend of mine, to write a book on Gung Fu techniques, which I have long forgotten. In order to fulfill his wish, I have included here in this book some of the basic techniques of the various schools of Gung Fu I have learned before my joining of the school of Wing Chung. It is true that the mental aspect of Gung Fu is the desired end; however, in order to achieve this stage, technical skill of the art has to come first.

I like to stress that this is <u>not</u> a textbook on Gung Fu formal techniques; rather, it is a book on some of the basic blocking and striking in that art. In the very near future, after my trip back from the Orient, a more thorough book entitled *The Tao of Chinese Gung Fu* will be published.

Since my three years stay in the U.S., I've seen unscrupulous "business men," Americans and Chinese alike, who claim themselves as professors or masters of Gung Fu and whose movements resemble nothing to any school in Gung Fu. I hope that people who are about to join these schools will examine them closely. I also would like to add that whoever reads this book will <u>not</u> be able to become a "holy terror"; nor can he become a Gung Fu expert in just three easy lessons.

B. Lee

PART 1
CHINESE MARTIAL ART

The Chinese martial art of Gung Fu basically consists of five "ways":

1 – Striking
(打法)
Includes all techniques of palms, fists, knees, elbows, shoulders, forearms, head and thighs, but does not include different schools' special techniques like the eagle claw, the beak of the crane, the mantis hand, etc.

2 – Kicking
(踢法)
Includes all types of techniques of kicking (both from Northern and Southern schools of China).

3 – Joint Locks
(擒拿)
Includes seventy-two techniques of different joint breaking and locking.

4 – Throwing
(摔法)
Includes thirty-six techniques of throwing.

5 – Weapons
(武器)
Includes eighteen different weapons.

There are innumerable schools of Gung Fu in both Northern and Southern parts of China. Among some of the well-known schools are:

<u>In Northern China</u> –

Wing Chung School (詠春派八扒),

Bart Kuar Clan (形意),

Ying Yee ([...]),

Northern Praying Mantis (螳螂),

Eagle Claw School (鷹爪派),

Tam Tuei (潭腿門),

Springing Leg (彈腿門),

Northern Sil Lum (北少林),

Law Hon (罗漢拳),

Lost Track School (迷踪藝),

Wa K'ung (西散華拳),

Ch'a K'ung (查拳),

Monkey Style (猴拳大聖門),

Chuiang Kung P'ai (長江派),

etc.

Publisher's Note: Unfortunately, Mr. Lee's Chinese character for Ying Yee has been lost.

In Southern China –

Wing Chung (咏春派),

Southern Praying Mantis (南派螳螂),

Dragon Style (白眉派),

White Crane School (白鶴派),

Southern Sil Lum (南派少林),

Choy Lay Fut (蔡李佛),

Hung K'ung (洪家),

Choy Ga (蔡家),

Fut Ga (佛家),

Mok Ga (莫家),

Yal Gung Moon (軟功門),

Li Ga (李家),

Lau Ga (劉家),

etc.

Then these clans are separated into so-called internal and external schools (內家与外家). Here we are not concerned with them.

SEVERAL IMPORTANT POINTERS

1. Every movement of Gung Fu has a flowing continuity without any dislocation. As soon as a movement is completed, it begins to flow into another one. Because of this, the readers will find the techniques of Gung Fu faster than the ordinary method.
2. Gung Fu is a mind exercise. The combination of mind and body is especially important in the higher stages of Gung Fu. As for the reader here, try to use the imagination (mental movement) to influence every physical movement; for example, a firm belief that every technique will come to the desired end would help.
3. Cooperate with your opponent. Do not resist or interrupt his flow of movement. Instead of stopping his force, complete it by following him. In other words, you help him to destroy himself. Remember this: What you will do depends on your opponent, which is why we say, "Be the complement and not the opposite of the opponent's force."
4. The waist is very important in the art of Gung Fu as it plays a major part in both striking and dissolving away the opponent's force. During practice, the practitioner is required to dissolve away the opponent's force by turning waist first before he can side step it. (Note: A white arrow will show the direction of turning of the waist in the illustrations.)
5. Remember, it is better to learn how to endure than to learn how to fight. However, if you are compelled to oppose force, make use of it.

BASIC GUNG FU STANCES

Gung Fu has many stances for different purposes, and some other schools have their own special stances. Here are the ten most commonly used stances for the beginners.

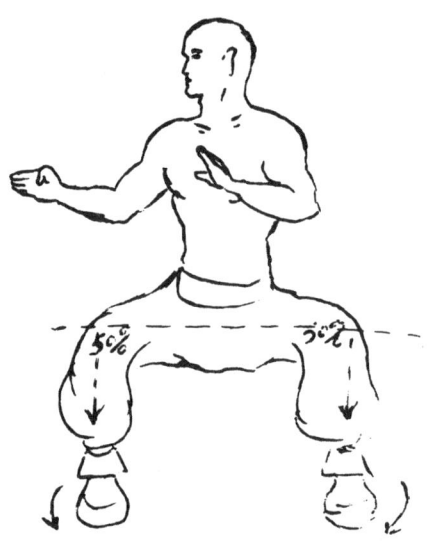

1 – Ma Bo (馬 步) – The thighs must be parallel, the toes point front and the knees point at the toes. The nearer the distance of the feet, the better.
<u>Points to Avoid</u> – Standing bow-legged or leaning forward or backward.

2 – Gung Bo (弓 步) – The weight is on the front leg with toes pointed slightly inward to avoid being stepped on; the back leg is straight. This is why this is sometimes called the bow and arrow stance. This stance and Ma Bo (horse stance) are strong and firm stances.

<u>Points to Avoid</u> – Lifting the heel up on the back foot or pointing the toes straight forward on the front foot.

3 – Ding Bo (丁 步) – Most of the weight is on the back leg, and the front leg stands with the toes pointing (ready to kick any time). The front knee is slightly higher than the back one for protection of the private parts.
<u>Points to Avoid</u> – Weight on front leg, toes not pointing straight.

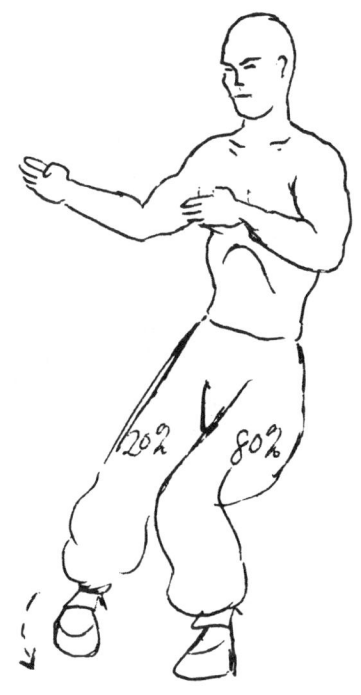

4 – Hui Bo (虛 步) – A slight variation of Ding Bo except with front toes turned slightly inward.
<u>Points to Avoid</u> – Weight on front foot.

5 – Chung Sik (中 式) – This is a medium stance between Ma Bo and Hui Bo and is mostly used in free-style sparring, due to its flexibility. The front knee is slightly higher than the rear one.

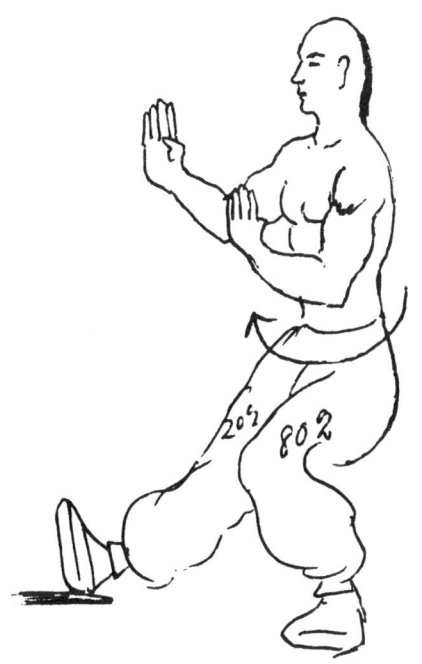

6 – Chuat Sing (七星) – Weight is on the back leg, and the front leg rests lightly on the heel with the toes pointing upward. This is mostly used with Gung Bo for dissolving away force. The waist plays a very important part in this stance. Both knees try to be parallel.

7 – Lau Ma (捋馬) – The twisting horse. The front foot is flat on the ground with the back heel raised. This stance is used mostly in close-range for moving with the shortest time.

8 – Kuai Ma (跪 馬) – The weight is on the front kneeing leg. This stance is used mostly for an attack to the low gate.

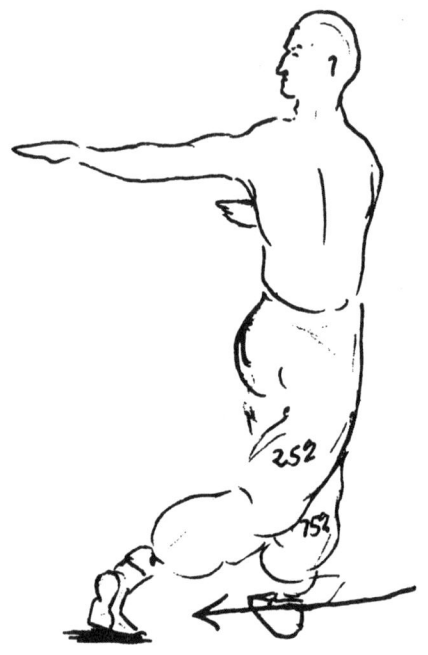

9 – Tou Bo (偷 步) – This stance in English means to steal a step or to sneak in to attack. From this stance, one can either kick or change it to many other stances like Ma Bo, Ding Bo, Gung Bo, etc.

10 – Tu Ma (吊 馬) – In English, it means hanging horse; this stance is for defense against foot sweeps, low kicks, weapon attacks, etc. From this position, a kick is often connected.

THE SEVEN STARS

Watch for the opponent's seven parts:

1) hands
2) feet
3) elbows
4) knees
5) shoulders
6) thighs
7) head

THE THREE FRONTS

Take care of one's "three fronts":

1) in front of one's eyes

2) in front of one's hands

3) in front of one's legs

ON WAIST TRAINING

The waist plays a vital role in the art of Gung Fu. Here are some exercises to extend the range of its motion and make the waist flexible.

Fig. 1 – Front Bend
(1) Bend forward with the palms touching the ground.
(2) The legs keep straight at all times.

Fig. 2
(1) Bend forward and grasp both ankles and touch the head on the knees.
(2) Later on, the head should touch the shin or, even better, the instep.

Fig. 3 – Side Bend
(1) Turn the body left and bend down without moving the lower trunk.
(2) Touch the palms on the ground.
(3) Come up and repeat the same to the right side.

Fig. 4 to Fig. 6 – Back Bend
Figures 4 to 6 show the steps toward back bending.

Fig. 6
(1) Stand with the feet together, the hands naturally raised and the body twisted toward the left side (Fig. 6A).
(2) The body turns from the left toward the right (Fig. 6B).
(3) The right hand turns to hook, and the left hand, following the turning of the waist, drops down and grasps the right ankle (Fig. 6C).
(4) The left hand releases and turns the body from right to left again.

Fig. 7

(1) From the standing position, the body drops toward the right side with the right foot crossing in front of the left foot (Fig. 7A).

(2) The body turns backward with the left foot grinding the ground and the right foot slightly touching the ground (Fig. 7B).

(3) After turning left, the foot bends slightly on the knee.

Fig. 8

(1) Assume a squatting position as in Fig. 8A with the left foot in front; the chest is close to the knee.

(2) The body turns toward the right back with the hand following (Fig. 8B).

(3) After turning the waist, the right leg should be in front as in Fig. 8B (dotted lines).

(4) Ready for left turning.

FIG 7·A   FIG 7B

FIG 8A   FIG 8B

ON LEG TRAINING

The kick, especially to the Northern clans of Gung Fu, is the best means of attack; however, they too warn of the danger of using it recklessly. It is a fact that the legs are much more powerful and have a longer reach than the hands, but we must consider also that when we lift one leg and kick, our whole balance is involved.

"In training, kick as high as you can; but in combat, kick as fast as you can and don't pass over the belt." This is a saying I often teach to my students. In my school, our kicks seldom pass over the belt, and the so-called high or flying kicks are never used. As for leg training, and this is true in most of the Gung Fu schools (North or South), it is not necessary for us to strengthen and toughen them by kicking on hard objects or sandbags. Due to their support of the whole body everyday, our legs already have power, and it is a matter of cultivating them <u>naturally</u>. The training then involves the cultivation and concentration of power and the development of speed.

Here I have included a few basic exercises that serve to develop kicking—the first part of which will concentrate on stretching the ligaments and extending the range of motion. The second part will be the natural development of kicking power.

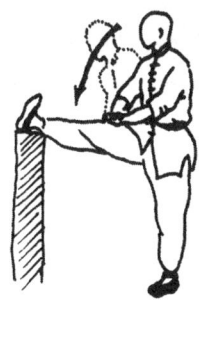 

Fig. 1   Fig. 2

Fig. 1 - Front Bend
Assume the position in Fig. 1 with the hands on the right knee to prevent it from bending. With the toes raised, try to touch the knee with the head. Repeat 15 times on each leg.

Fig. 2 - Side Bend
Assume the position in Fig. 2 with the hands on the hips. With the toes raised, bend sideways and touch the right foot with the head.

Fig. 3A   Fig. 3B

Fig. 3A to Fig. 3B
This exercise is commonly called shoe kissing. (1) Assume a squatting position with the left leg extending straight, the toes raised and the heel touching the ground. (2) With two hands grasping the left foot and pulling backward, bend forward and kiss the shoe. Practice left and right. NOTE: At first, practice by touching the head on the knees, then reach farther and farther out.

FIG 4A   FIG 4B

Fig. 4A to Fig. 4B

Assume the same position; but this time, bend over and try to touch the shoe with the head. (This time the right side of the body touches the left leg.) Repeat 12–20 times and do the same with the right leg.

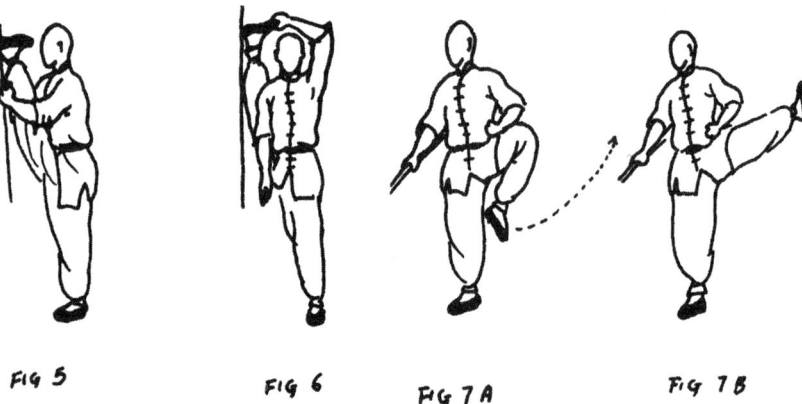

FIG 5   FIG 6   FIG 7A   FIG 7B

Fig. 5 to Fig. 6

Fig. 5 and Fig. 6 show a slightly more difficult exercise of leg training.

Fig. 7A to Fig. 7B – Side Hang

This exercise is known as leg hanging in Chinese because, when the leg is raised to the desired position, it has to stop there for as long as one can. (1) Assume the position in Fig. 7A with the right hand on a bar. (2) Slowly lift the left leg (with toes raised) to around 90° from the ground and stay there for a while. (3) Lower it down to the original position and repeat the same procedure again.

Fig. 8A to Fig. 8B – Straight Hang
(1) Assume the original position. (2) This time, instead of raising the leg sideways, raise it slowly straight up (toe raised) till it reaches at least 90° from the ground. (3) Stay there for a while and repeat again.

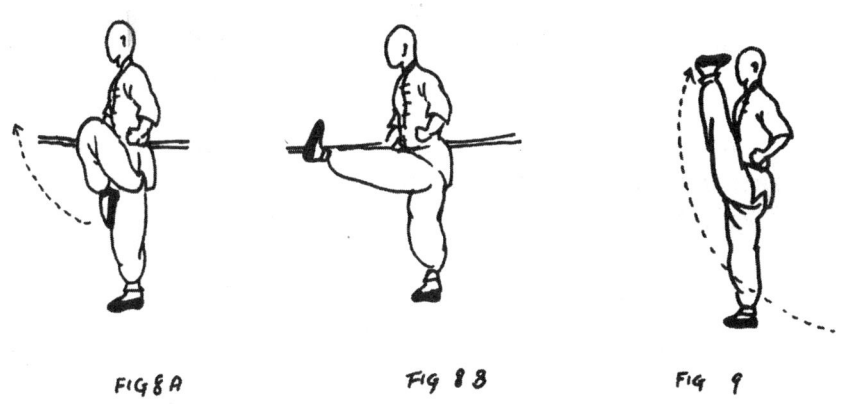

FIG 8A   Fig 8B   Fig 9

Fig. 9
This is a front high kick for practicing purposes only. (1) With hands on the hips, advance the right foot with the left foot behind it. (2) The left foot kicks up straight with toes raised, aiming at one's forehead. (3) When the left foot comes down next to the right foot, stop and advance the left foot with the right foot behind, ready to kick.
NOTE: (1) During kicking, the waist should not bend, and do not lean forward too much.
(2) The body should not bend backward.
(3) The stationary foot should be firmly flat on the ground.

Fig. 10 – Side Slanting Kick

(1) Assume the same position as in Fig. 9 and kick with the left leg the same way except to the side of the right ear. (2) The hand-extending position is for balancing the posture of the body.

Fig. 11 – Side Straight Kick

(1) From an erect position, advance the right foot with the toes slightly pointing to the right side; the body is also turned toward the right side as shown in Fig. 11. (2) The left foot kicks toward the left ear. (3) The left foot lands on the ground with the toes pointing slightly toward the left side and the body turning toward the left side.
(4) Kick in the same manner.

Fig. 12 to Fig. 14

(1) Fig. 12 and Fig. 14 show the exercise of leg swinging in an out and inward swing. Practice with the left and right leg. (2) Fig. 13 shows the correct posture while swinging the leg.

Fig. 15 to Fig. 17

This is the actual kicking as used in actual application. Here I have just included three basic kicks in Gung Fu: the side kick, the thrust kick and the straight-toe kick.

Fig. 15 – Side Kick

(1) Assume the position in Fig. 15 with the body erect. (2) Advance the right foot and snap out the left foot like a whip with all the power concentrating on impact. (3) Snap back as fast as possible and land in front of the right foot. (4) In the same manner, the right foot snaps out.

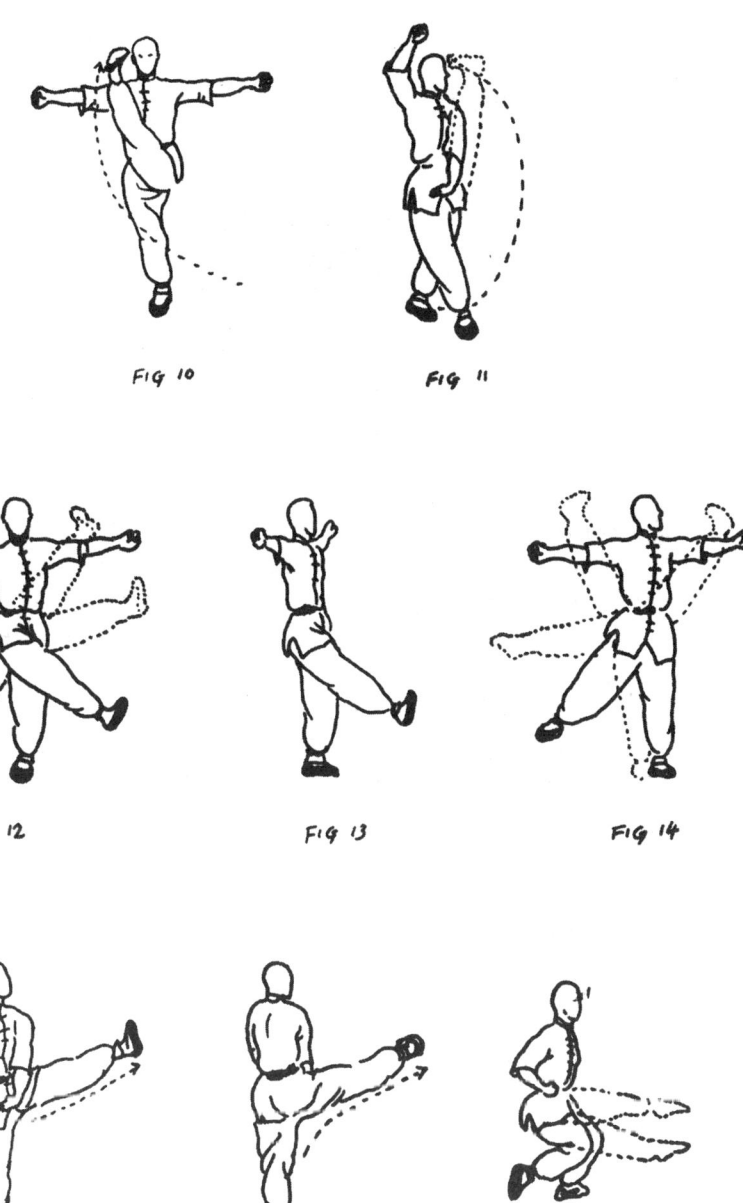

THE BASIC THEORY OF YIN AND YANG IN THE ART OF GUNG FU

At first, I did not plan to include this section as the book deals only with basic techniques; however, on second thought, I believe the reader will be greatly benefited by this Chinese view of life. Most likely his technique (no matter what system he is in) will also be greatly improved.

The basic structure of Gung Fu is based on the theory of Yin/Yang (陰 陽), a pair of mutually complementary forces that act continuously, without cessation, in this universe. This Chinese way of life can be applied to anything, but here we are interested in its relationship to the art of Gung Fu. The black part of the circle is called Yin (陰). Yin can represent anything in the universe such as negativeness, passiveness, gentleness, insubstantiality, femaleness, moon, darkness, night, etc. The other complementary part of the circle is Yang (陽), which represents positiveness, activeness, firmness, substantiality, maleness, sun, brightness, day, etc.

The common mistake most people make is to identify this Yin/Yang symbol, T'ai-Chi (太 極), as dualistic—that is, Yang being the opposite of Yin and vice versa. As long as we separate this "oneness" into two, we won't achieve realization. Actually, all things have their complementary part; it is only in the human mind and his perception that they are being separated into opposites. The sun is not the opposite of the moon as they complement and are interdependent on each other, and we cannot survive without either of them. In a similar way, a male is but the complement of the female; for without the male, how on earth do we know there is female or vice versa? The "oneness" of Yin/Yang is necessary in life. If a person riding a bicycle wishes to go somewhere, he cannot pump on both pedals at the same time or not pump on them at all. In order to move forward, he has to pump one pedal and release the other. So the movement of going forward requires this "oneness" of pumping and releasing. Pumping then is the result of releasing and vice versa—each being the cause of the other.

In the Yin/Yang symbol, there is a white spot on the black part and a black spot on the white one. This is to illustrate the balance in life, for nothing can survive long by going to either extremes—be it negativeness or positiveness. Therefore, firmness must be concealed in gentleness and gentleness in firmness, which is why a Gung Fu man must be pliable as a spring. Notice that the stiffest tree is most easily cracked, while the bamboo will bend with the wind. So in Gung Fu, or any other system, one must be gentle yet not giving away completely; be firm yet not hard; and even if he is strong, he should guard it with softness and tenderness. For if there is no softness in firmness, he is not strong; in a similar way, if one has firmness concealed in softness, no one can break through his defense. This principle of moderation provides the best means of preserving oneself, for since we accept this existence of oneness (Yin/Yang) in everything, and do not treat it dualistically, we thus secure a state of tranquility by remaining detached and not inclining to either extreme. Even if we do incline on one extreme, be it negative or positive, we will flow with it in order to control it. This flowing with it, without clinging, is the true way to get rid of it.

When the movements in Yin/Yang flow into extremes, reaction sets in. For when Yang goes to the extreme, it changes to Yin; and when Yin (activated by Yang) goes to the extreme, it returns back to Yang. That is why each one is the result and cause of the other. For example, when one works to the extreme, he becomes tired and has to rest (from Yang to Yin). After resting, he can work again (Yin back to Yang). This incessant changing of Yin/Yang is always continuous.

The application of the theory of Yin/Yang in Gung Fu is known as the Law of Harmony in which one should be in harmony with, and not against, the force of the opponent. Suppose A applies strength on B; B shouldn't oppose or give way completely to it. For these are but the two extreme opposites of B's reaction. Instead, he should <u>complete</u> A's force with a lesser force, and lead him to the direction of his own movement. As the butcher preserves his knife by cutting along the bone and not against it, a Gung Fu man preserves himself by following the movement of his opponent without opposition or even striving (Wu-Wei 無 為 – spontaneous or spirit action). This spontaneous assisting of A's movement as he aims it will result in his own defeat.

When a Gung Fu man finally understands the theory of Yin/Yang, he no longer "fusses" with so-called "gentleness" or "firmness"; he simply does what the moment requires him to do. In fact, all conventional forms and techniques are all gone; his movements are those of everyday movements. He doesn't have to "justify" himself like so many other masters have, claiming his spirit or internal power; to him, cultivation of a martial art in the long run will return to simplicity, and only people of half-way cultivation will justify and brag about themselves.

PART 2

CHINESE GUNG FU TECHNIQUES

1-A

1-B

1-C

1-A A comes in with a straight left punch in Gung Bo (bow and arrow stance 弓 步).

1-B Turning his waist, B dissolves A's punch in an upward arc. Unlike other schools of blocking with power, a Gung Fu block tends to dissolve the oncoming force and return it back to the opponent. (Note: The white arrow indicates the direction of turning of the waist.)

1-C Continuing his motion, B follows with a finger jab to the attacker's eye. Notice the other hand is on guard. (Note: After constant practice, the blocking and striking should be one continuous action.)

2-A

2-B

2–C

2-A   A leads with a straight left punch.

2-B   B steps in with Chung Sik (medium stance 中式), simultaneously deflects the punch with a left slapping hand (左拍手) and strikes the opponent with a right knuckle fist (右插捶).

2 C   A thrusts out his right hand, and B, without changing his position, blocks it with his left and at the same time jabs A's throat with an upward finger poke from where his right hand was (右插喉掌).

3-A

3-A   A leads with a right punch.

3-B

3-B At the slightest movement of A, B steps back, blocks and side kicks his opponent at the same time (右側摔腿). (Notice B's right hand is in position.)

4-A

4-B

4-C

4-A   A comes in with a right hook.

4-B   B side steps and, turning his waist, blocks and jabs his opponent's eyes simultaneously.

4-C   A again comes in with a left upper cut to the midsection. B side steps and at the same time slashes down his right hand and again jabs A with left finger thrusts (標 指).

5-A

5-B

5-C

5-A A grasps B's hands.

5-B B advances his right foot and at the same time strikes A's right wrist bone by his own left thumb.

5-C After A releases the grip, B then punches his face with a straight left (冲捶).

6-A

6-B

6–C

6–A A bear-hugs B from the rear. B relaxes and sinks down his weight.

6–B, C Turning his waist, B strikes A with his elbow and at the same time steps on his toes.

7-A

7-A   A comes in with a straight right in a left Gung Bo.

7-B

7-B   B side steps, deflects the punch and strikes A's ribs with a knuckle fist (插 捶).

8-A

8-A   A comes in with a right side kick
      (右側撐腿).

8-B

8-B B comes down (in an arc) with a hand hook (notice his left hand is on guard) and counters by kicking A's groin with a straight toe kick (直挑腿).

9-A

9-B

9-C

9-A   A pushes B.

9-B   B, turning his waist and advancing, deflects and strikes A with a knuckle fist (指 槌) as shown in the picture.

9-C   Turning his right hand in an arc to lead the oncoming movement of the opponent, B skips in and strikes him with the knee.

10-A

10-B

10–C

10–A, B   A comes in with a lunging straight right punch.

10–C   Without backing up, B turns his waist and leads the opponent to the direction of his own movement.

10-D

10-D   A intends to pull each right punch and snap out his left.

10-E

10-E At the slightest movement of withdrawal, B follows, slaps down and locks both of A's arms; at the same time, B strikes A with a straight right.

11-A

11-B

11-C

11-A, B   A intends to throw B as shown in pictures 11-A and 11-B. (There are, by the way, 36 throwing techniques and 72 joint locks in the art of Gung Fu.)

11-C   Turning his waist, B grasps A's left hand and at the same time turns his shoulder out and downward against A's shoulder.

11-D

11-D   By kicking his right foot sharply into a Gung Bo, B counters A by throwing him.

11-E

11-E　　Either a knee or fist can follow to finish the opponent.

12-A

12-A   Opponent A steps in with a straight finger jab.

12-B

12-B   Without backing up, B leads A's force by turning his waist and at the same time strikes A with the edge of the hand. (Acknowledgement: Mr. Charles Woo, the defender, by the way, is a 2nd degree black belt holder in Judo.)

13-A

13-A   A leads with a straight right. B deflects with his right hand. (Notice the left hand on guard.)

13-B

13-B   A withdraws his right hand and shoots out his left to B's midsection. B simply slaps the punch downward with his left and jabs A's eyes with his right from his previous position.

14-A

14-A   A comes in with a left. B deflects the punch with a right hand hook.

14-B

14-B A withdraws his left and shoots out his right. B deflects the oncoming punch with his left hand (in the form of an arc) and, following A's withdrawal of energy, he strikes A with a right knuckle fist (from the previous hooking position).

15-A

15-A   Right at this moment X doesn't concentrate on any of his opponents' actions; he simply has a quiet awareness of the immediate situation without thinking of the outcome or anything.

15-B

15-A, B Opponent A attacks X with a right hook. X, turning his waist, blocks and jabs A with a right. (Notice the changing of footwork.)

15-C

15-B, C As X disables A, B comes in with a straight punch. From where he is, X turns his waist, deflects it and side kicks B.

15-D

15-C, D At this moment, C lunges in with a straight right to the face. X dissolves the punch in an arc and at the same strikes him with a knuckle fist.

16-A

16-B

16-C

16-A, B   A steps in with a right straight heart punch. X deflects the punch and counters with a back fist (掛 捶) to A's temple. At this moment, B comes in.

16-B, C   X sweeps his left hand back in an arc and slides in with a kneeing horse (Kuai Ma) and strikes B's groin as shown in the pictures.

17-A

17-A   A comes in with a straight knuckle fist to the solar plexus.

17-B

17-A, B   B, turning his waist, hooks A's punch and counters with a straight knuckle fist.

18-A

18-A   A and B facing in ready position.

18–B

18–A, B   A comes in with a finger jab to B's throat. B leads A's movement by turning his waist. This dissolving is not by the hand but by the waist so as to really unbalance the oncoming force as he makes it.

19-A

19-B

19–C

19–A   A and B stand in natural position as A applies pressure on B's hand.

19–B   B assists A by jerking him to the direction of his force and at the same time skips in with a straight thrust kick. (Notice the left hand is in position.)

19–B, C   A blocks B's straight kick with his left. B, by following the direction of A's blocking, turns and kicks A's knee with a low side thrust kick.

DIFFERENCE IN GUNG FU STYLES

The technique of a superior system of Gung Fu is based on simplicity. It is only the half-cultivated systems that are full of unnecessary wasted motions.

Simplicity is the natural result of profound and long study of the <u>way</u> of movements. A good Gung Fu man is a simplifier.

Here are some examples of a slower system against the more effective Gung Fu techniques.

100

Fig. 100   A advances with "pow chuie," an uppercut blow.

101

Fig 101   B, without wasted motions, simply hooks down with his left hand and strikes A's carotid artery by following his withdrawing energy.

200

201

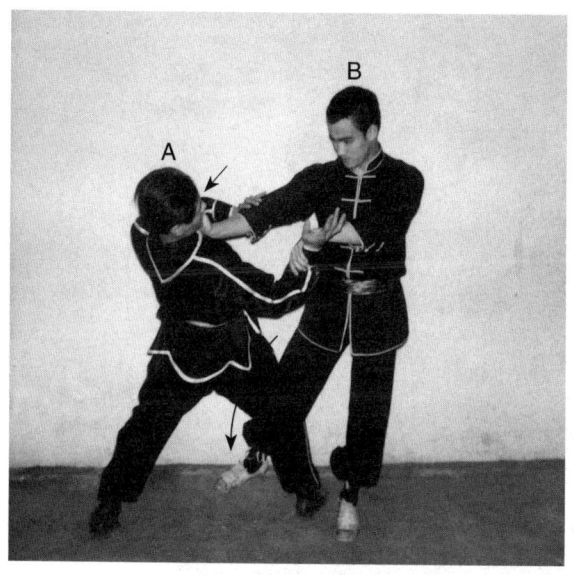

202

Fig. 200   In Gung Fu, one never grabs someone as shown. For illustration, let's assume that B grabs A's clothing.

Fig. 200 to 201   A advances his right foot and attempts a right upward elbow strike. It is dangerous to use the elbow in the far-range; as you can see during A's advance, B can simply punch straight (Fig. 201). Elbows should be reserved for close-range combat.

Fig. 202   B continues the action, throws A with a cross hook throw and simultaneously strikes A's jaw with the heel of a hand blow.

300

Fig. 300 When grabbed by somebody, instead of applying a joint lock or pushing him off-balance, one is better off by simply kicking his attacker on the shin or, if his other hand is free, just punching him.

Let's assume B grabs A's hand, and A tries to unbalance B's posture by advancing his right foot and at the same time pushing B's elbow toward his own body.

301

Fig. 301   During the process of all these movements, B can either kick A's groin while he advances or just jab at his eye. Or, as shown in Fig. 301, B comes in with both a hand jab and a toe kick.

400

Fig. 400 A grasps B's hand and pulls him in for a left side elbow to the ribs.

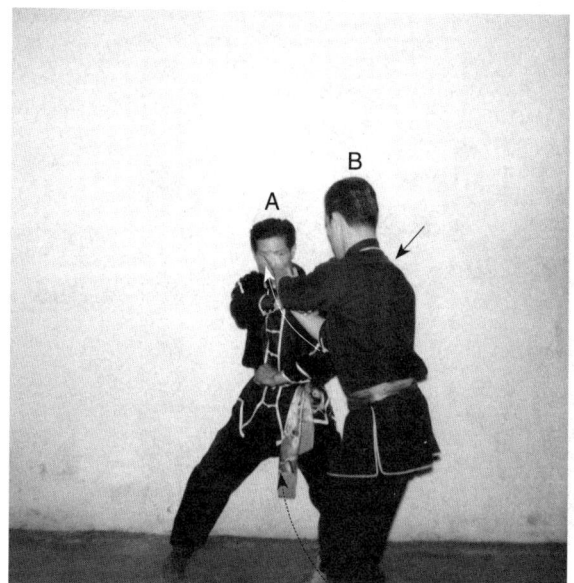

401

Fig. 401 B simply drops his elbow and, following in an arc facing A, strikes him at the same time with his left finger jab, but a straight kick can also follow.

500

501

502

Fig. 500 B comes in with a straight right, and A, in twisting horse, deflects B's punch.

Fig. 501 Advancing into a horse stance slightly toward the right side of B, A is ready for a side hand chop to B's ribs. Actually, B can now come in by a finger jab or edge of the hand by checking A's elbow with his left hand.

Fig. 502 As A comes in, B, in the same position, deflects the punch with his right hand and counters with a right hook kick.

PART 3
ADDITIONAL TECHNIQUES

INTRODUCTION
By Shannon Lee

It was a difficult decision whether to include the following pictures and annotations as an extra section within the pages of this book. It was difficult because obviously these pictures were not originally intended for this book and also because we had very little information on the origin and intent of these photos.

It seems clear that had my father wished to include these in a revised edition of this book or any other, then he would have. It also seems clear, however, that at some point in time he did take these pictures and annotate them with the idea of a book in mind. Whether he ever finished the photos and text for this new book idea or whether his evolution just took him away from the idea behind this book altogether, we will never know.

As my mother mentioned in her foreword at the beginning of the book, my father eventually moved away from the continued publication of *Chinese Gung Fu* as his beliefs about the martial arts evolved. Time, however, has shown that the evolutionary steps and rudimentary knowledge of Bruce Lee continue to be of great interest to the martial arts world. It is for this reason that we chose not only to reprint *Chinese Gung Fu* but also to include more material that offers an insight into my father's evolution and base of knowledge.

The photos and annotations that are in this section do not make up the pages of a complete volume or even a complete thought. Rather, these are a collection of photos and notes that are more of a glimpse into the process of Bruce Lee's martial experience. They are presented to you in raw form because we, and the editors, did not want to assume any kind of interpretation. We hope you will find these pages as interesting as we do and will take the time to look through them with a thorough eye toward the martial art they impart. In his desire to teach, my father was the consummate student. If nothing else, these pages stand as a testament to a man who was passionate about the martial arts and who wanted to share his experience with others.

S. Lee
2008

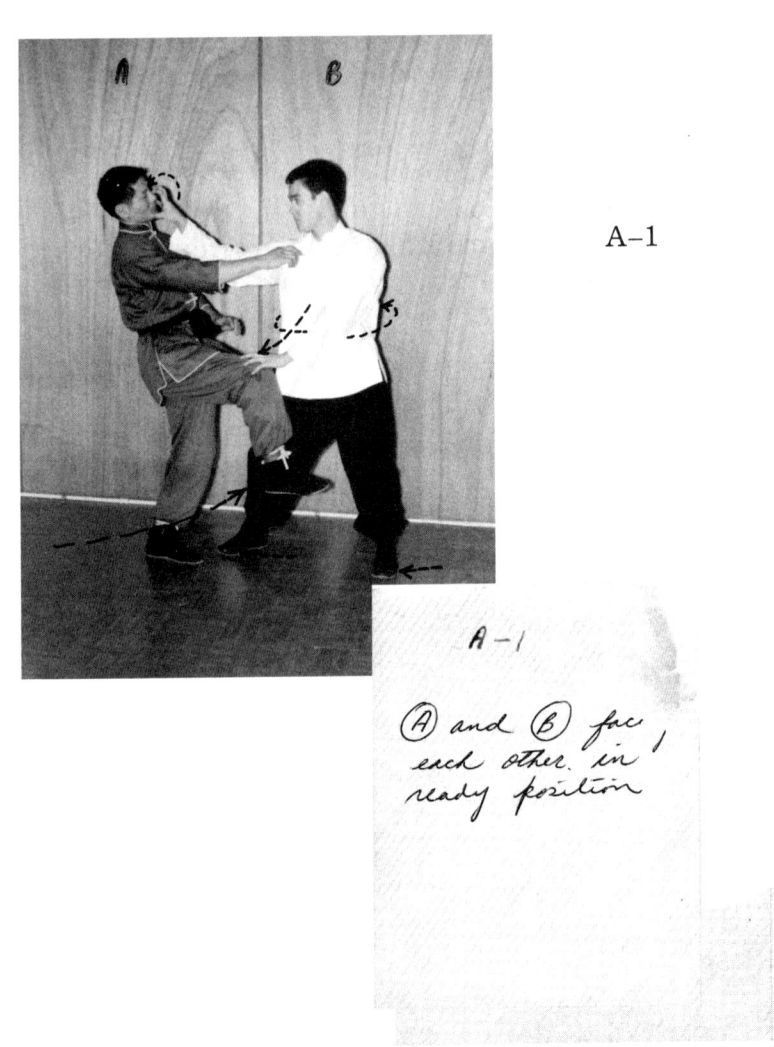

A-1   A and B face each other in ready position.

A–2   In ONE moti[on], A locks B's [right] hand and strikes his throat simultaneously. (Note the locking of B's leg for prevention of kicks.)

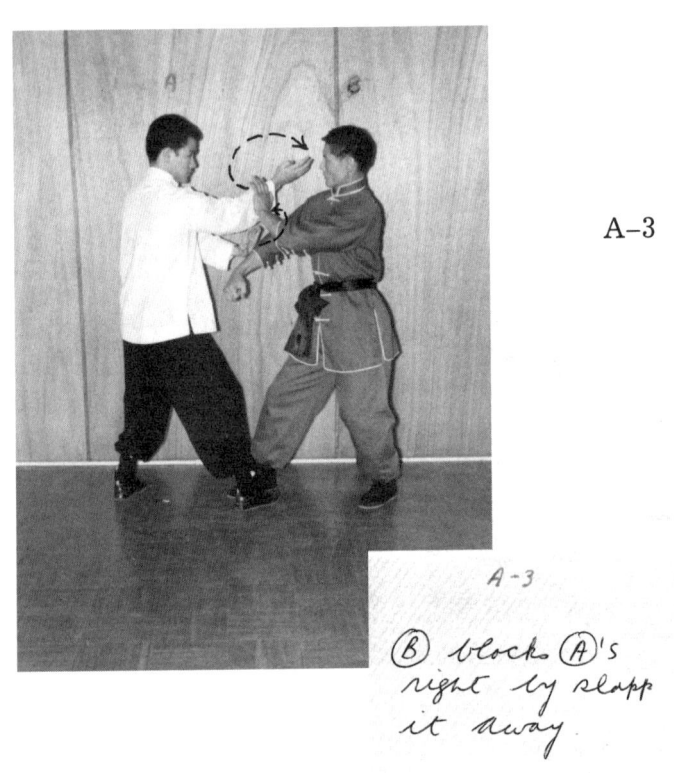

A-3

A-3   B blocks A's right by slap[ping] it away.

A-4   Flowing with B, [...] slapping hand without resisting. A traps B's left hand and counter[s] with a back fist.

A-5

A-5

Closing in, A comes in with two straight p[unches] as shown in the following two pictures. [observe how B is "locked" without any striking or kicking room]

A-6

A–5, 6 Closing in, [A] comes in with two straignt [punches] as shown in the following two pictures. (Observe how B is "locked" without any striking or kicking room.)

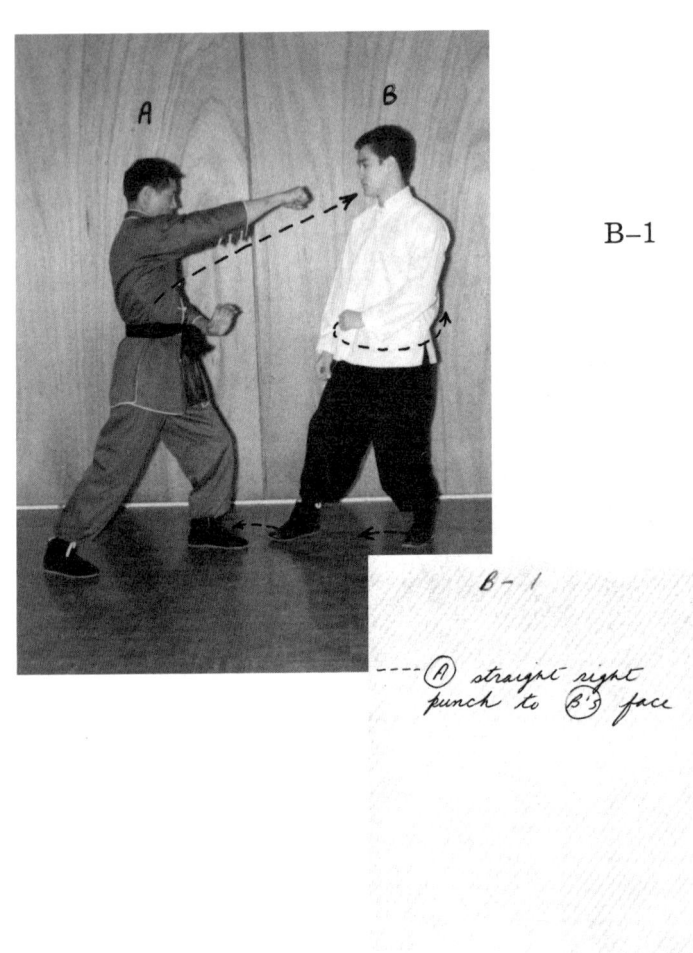

B-1

B-1   A straight right punch[es] to B's face.

B-2

B-2 Advancing, B deflects A's punch and strike[s] him simultaneously by turning his waist. The deflection should be outward and upward without over-reaching, thus going off the body.

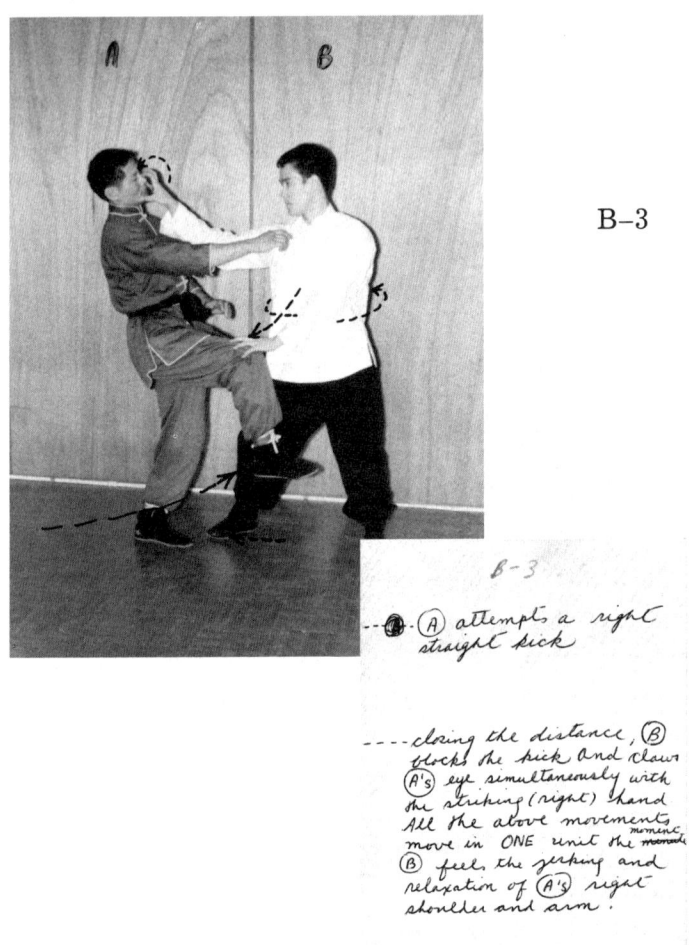

B-3

B-3   A attempts a right straight kick. Closing the distance, B blocks the kick and claws A's eye simultaneously with the striking (right) hand. All the above movements move in ONE unit the moment B feel[s] the jerking and relaxation of A's right shoulder and arm.

C-1

C-1   This is a classical Gung Fu technique. A right straight punch[es] in [a] bow and arrow stance. B right forearm block[s].

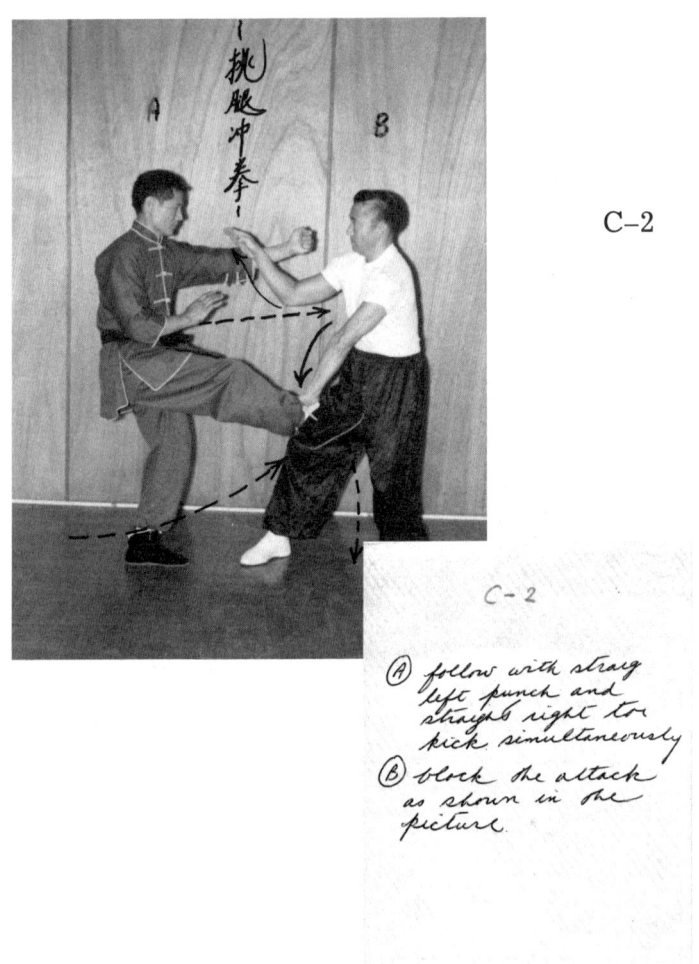

C-2

C-2   A follows with [a] straig[ht] left punch and [a] straight right toe kick simultaneously. B block[s] the attack as shown in the picture.

C-3 Just before the right foot touches the [ground], A move[s] in with a right solar plexus punch, ending in a horse stance. (Note: A's left hand [is] on guard—also, his right foot is locking B's to prevent his kick.)

B blocks A's punch as shown.

C-4   Following B's downward movement, A slaps B's right elbow and counter[s] with a right back fist (all in one motion). Note that the distance is closed and A's right foot is locking B's.

D (One picture only.) The straight finger jab is used when the opponent attempts to strike, bringing his hand out of the center line. This finger jab can also be successfully used against an opponent who feints or swings wildly. A simple but practical technique; you will be amazed how a simple finger jab like this can interrupt and upset your opponent's fancy mess.

E-1

Publisher's Note: Because Mr. Lee left no annotations behind for photos E-1 through E-6, we are leaving them in their original format.

E-2

E-3

 E-4

E-5

E-6

The following are some photos taken at Ralph Castro's Kenpo Karate Studio in San Francisco during a visit. It shows the author (left) and Ed Parker in Bi Jong, or ready position.

From left to right: Author, Ed Parker, James Lee and Ralph Castro.

Publisher's Note: Ed Parker and Ralph Castro were black belt Kenpo Karate instructors.

From left to right: Author with Ed Parker and James Y. Lee during Gung Fu gabfest.

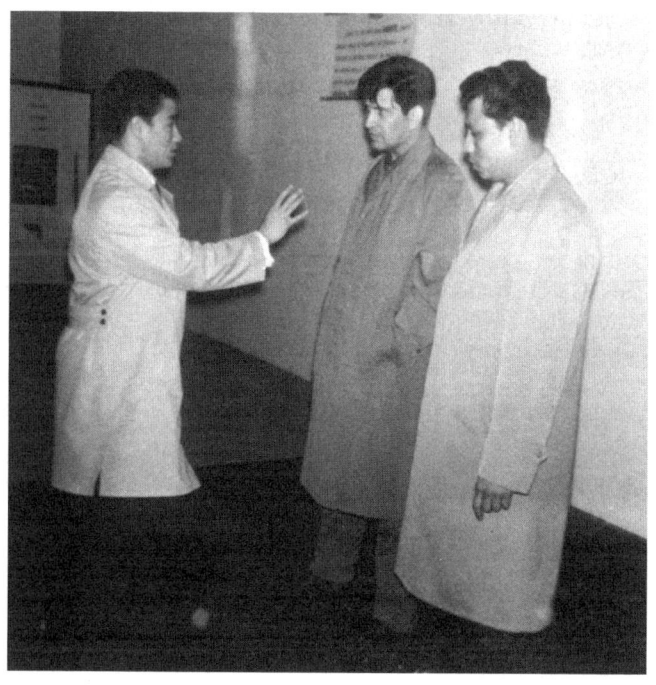

From left to right: Author with Ed Parker and Ralph Castro in Castro's spacious studio.

图书在版编目（CIP）数据

李小龙基本中国拳法 /（美）李小龙著；黄筠译. ——北京：北京联合出版公司，2015.9（2022.10重印）
 ISBN 978-7-5502-6261-4

Ⅰ.①李… Ⅱ.①李…②黄… Ⅲ.①截拳道—运动技术 Ⅳ.①G886.9

中国版本图书馆CIP数据核字（2015）第222627号

CHINESE GUNG FU:THE PHILOSOPHICAL ART OF SELF-DEFENSE
By
BRUCE LEE
Copyright © 2008 Bruce Lee Enterprises，LLC.
This edition arranged with INDEPENDENT PUBLISHERS GROUP（IPG）through Big Apple Agency，Inc.，Labuan，Malaysia.
Simplified Chinese edition copyright © 2015 POST WAVE PUBLISHING CONSULTING（Beijing）Ltd.
All rights reserved.
本书中文简体版权归属于后浪出版咨询(北京)有限责任公司

李小龙基本中国拳法

著　　者：李小龙
译　　者：黄　筠
出 品 人：赵红仕
选题策划：后浪出版公司
出版统筹：吴兴元
特约编辑：张　怡
责任编辑：王　巍
封面设计：周伟伟
营销推广：ONEBOOK
装帧制造：墨白空间

北京联合出版公司出版
（北京市西城区德外大街83号楼9层　100088）
天津中印联印务有限公司印刷　新华书店经销
字数136千字　889毫米×1194毫米　1/32　8.5印张　插页2
2016年1月第1版　2022年10月第11次印刷
ISBN 978-7-5502-6261-4
定价：32.00元

后浪出版咨询(北京)有限责任公司　版权所有，侵权必究
投诉信箱：copyright@hinabook.com　　fawu@hinabook.com
未经许可，不得以任何方式复制或者抄袭本书部分或全部内容
本书若有印、装质量问题，请与本公司联系调换，电话010-64072833

生活的艺术家

作　　者：李小龙
编辑整理：约翰·里特
译　　者：刘军平
书　　号：978-7-5502-1350-0
定　　价：32.00元

李小龙传世遗作震撼面世
梁文道《开卷八分钟》诚意推荐

他是战无不胜的功夫之王，
却深谙玄妙的东方哲学，用无为的道家思想诠释功夫的真谛。
他是叱咤风云的好莱坞巨星，
却厌倦浮华喧嚣的名利场，在宁静的自我思省中探求人生的真理。
翻开本书，你会遇见一个不一样的李小龙。

西方人对李小龙的认识，是已经把他抬到一个哲学家的地步了。

——梁文道《开卷八分钟》

在这里，小龙剥掉了他内心灵魂的层层外衣，向世界展示他的真我。

——琳达·李·卡德维尔，李小龙夫人

李小龙是许多人的偶像，其伟大之处在于他激励着千百万年经人追随他的足迹。

——施瓦辛格

截拳道之道
（全新修订版）

作　者：李小龙
译　者：杜子心　罗振光
书　号：978-7-5502-3309-6
定　价：68.00元（平装）
　　　　128.00元（精装）

李小龙传世遗作震撼面世　梁文道《开卷八分钟》诚意推荐

最具影响力的李小龙武学名著
永不过时的截拳道理论经典
深度揭示《李小龙技击法》的精神内核
全球首次授权中文版

《截拳道之道》是一本非常独特的书，因为它是传达李小龙截拳道武术精髓的文章的有机汇集。它不是一本关于"如何练成"的书。此书是一个异数。

——李香凝，李小龙之女

每次翻开《截拳道之道》，我会在脑海中浮现李小龙卷曲书籍、手执笔杆的画面。我对于他在人类身、心、灵方面的探索所下的工夫感到惊讶。

——琳达·李·卡德韦尔，李小龙遗孀

《截拳道之道》事实上是永无止境的。这本书也只能作为读者的一个开端，它是无形、没有层级的。……你会发觉，截拳道并没有任何明确的界线或界限，除非你划地自限。

——吉尔伯特·约翰逊，《截拳道之道》编者